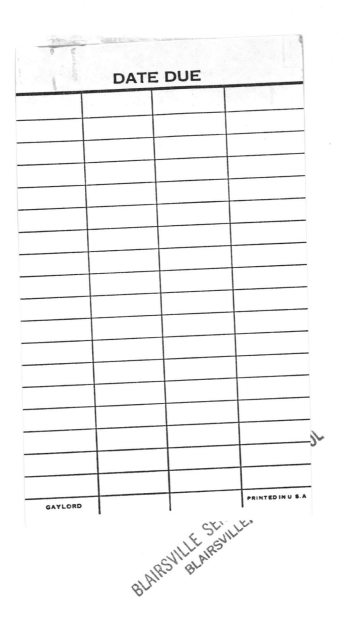

DATE DUE

GAYLORD

PRINTED IN U.S.A

FINDING
YOUR WAY

FINDING YOUR WAY
A BOOK ABOUT SEXUAL ETHICS

BY SUSAN NEIBURG TERKEL

WITH ILLUSTRATIONS
BY SARAH DURHAM

FRANKLIN WATTS
A DIVISION OF GROLIER PUBLISHING
NEW YORK / LONDON / HONG KONG / SYDNEY
DANBURY, CONNECTICUT

This book is dedicated to my daughter,
Marni Anne Terkel

Portions of the text have been adapted from material previously published in *Applied Ethics*, a college text, copyright © 1993 by St. Petersburg Junior College, and are reprinted with permission by St. Petersburg Junior College and McGraw-Hill, Inc.

Acknowledgments
The author would like to thank Lorna Greenberg, her editor, for her dedication and unswerving faith in the project, and her agent, Kendra Marcus. Gratitude also to Michael L. Richardson, Karen K. White, Ph.D., Janice Rench, Kara Reilly, Jennifer Joy Glasier, Bernice Massey, Kari Carney, Dan Fromm, Margaret Pepe, Ph.D., Pam Brubocker, Ph.D., Ira Reiss, Ph.D., Vince Bushnell, Rev. Ron Duer, Sarah Johnson, Mark Osgood, Alexis Georgopoulos, Jill Stefano, Joy Wilson, and most of all, my children, Marni, Ari, and Dave, and my husband, Larry, who discussed the topic endlessly.

Library of Congress Cataloging-in-Publication Data

Terkel, Susan Neiburg.
    Finding your way : a book about sexual ethics / by Susan Neiburg Terkel : with illustrations by Sarah Durham.
        p. cm.
    Includes bibliographical references and index.
    Summary: Discusses sexual ethics and morality to help young people make critical and educated decisions about their sexual behavior.
    ISBN 0-531-11234-9
    1. Sexual ethics for teenagers—Juvenile literature. [Sexual ethics.] I. Durham, Sarah, ill. II. Title.
HQ32.T47   1995
306.7'0835—dc20   95-16828
                                                              CIP AC

CONTENTS

IN THE COMPANY OF EROS

Billy Sheahan scored 67 points. Not on a test. Or for golf, basketball, or football. Sheahan "earned" a point for each girl with whom he had sexual intercourse. And many other boys in his "league" at Lakewood High School in Lakewood, California, scored points in the same manner. When the scandal hit the news and talk show circuit, it earned the school a reputation for the moral decay of its student body.

Points were earned by having sexual intercourse, and some members of the Spur Posse, as the group was known, achieved this through sexual harassment and rape. Some scored with girls as young as ten years old. As Robert Ripley, a detective involved in the case observed, "There was no foreplay, there was no romance, there was no sweet-talking. It was strictly drop your drawers and let's get with it."[1]

True, a few girls willingly participated. Others consented out of fear that if they resisted, the boys would harm them even more. While this particular brand of scorekeeping and sexual intimidation remains something of an anomaly on the high school landscape, it nonetheless signals a common attitude that sex is a game of conquest and popularity. Most of all, the Spur Posse is a vestige of the double standard that says "nice girls don't." And because they don't, "bedding" a nice girl signifies success. The double standard also justifies such behavior on the (mistaken) belief that adolescent boys have "rampaging hormones" and a unique urgency for sex.

Sheahan clearly wronged those whom he forced to have sex against their will. He also offended and enraged many people in the general public, who were appalled by the Spur Posse's behavior. Surprisingly, though, a number of people, particularly the fathers of teenage sons, came to Sheahan's defense.

Why were Billy Sheahan and his comrades so guilty of sexual indecency? How could they justify making sex a contest, or striving to have so many sexual partners a game? And why did members of the Spur Posse fail to consider how their conduct would affect others, or cast a cloud over their school's reputation?

It's easy to pass judgment on someone else's sexual behavior and morality, especially on behavior as reprehensible as that of the Spur Posse. But upholding our own standards—or finding suitable ones in the first place—is a formidable challenge for anyone.

One of the first steps to understanding *ethics* is to become aware of the behavior, situations, and dilemmas that have a moral aspect. *Sexual ethics* involves considering our sexual behavior. In our society, as in most societies, sexual behavior is steeped in custom and morality. Because our society allows us the freedom to think and choose for ourselves, people have many different ideas and opinions about what is sexually moral and what is immoral. An example of this occurred when former Surgeon General Jocelyn Elders made a statement in 1994 about masturbation.[2] Many people were outraged by her opinion that masturbation is acceptable (and even preferable to other kinds of sexual behavior at times), and Dr. Elders was compelled to resign amid a storm of criticism, whereas others, perhaps less vocal, did not find her remarks objectionable.

Through the study of ethics, a person can learn how to think critically and make educated decisions about his or her behavior. Ethics also helps people make moral judgments about the behavior of other people as well. Making a moral judgment is not the same as being judgmental or closed-minded, however. Rather, it allows us to recognize and decide to stop behavior that is truly wrong, such as sexual harassment, and make room for positive changes in our customs, such as encouraging people to be more responsible about preventing sexually transmitted diseases and unwanted pregnancies.

In between the black and white areas of moral judgment are the many gray ones, where people cannot agree, such as about masturbation, nonmarital sex, or teenage access to birth control and sexual education. By learning more about both sides of these issues, people can come closer to resolving their differences about them

ALL THINGS CONSIDERED

In this book, you will read about many subjects dealing with sex, all of which deal with sexual morality—and how a person can enjoy sex without stepping on the rights of others or getting hurt or hurting someone else. Besides personal ethics, you will also read about public issues, such as the extent to which public figures are entitled to privacy about their sexual affairs and preferences.

It is important to read this book with an open mind and to re-member that you don't have to agree with the author in order to gain from the material presented. In fact, the tradition of ethics is one of continuous probing, debate, analysis, and learning—indeed, all that is exciting about ethical inquiry. Besides demonstrating how to think about sexual issues more clearly, though, reading about sexual ethics can help you become a better person by inspiring you to act more kindly and responsibly, and to take a moral stand for what you believe is right.

To keep the book a manageable length, some topics have been omitted—not because they aren't important, but because they would require an entire book to themselves. Others were not aired because they were not as pertinent to teenagers as the topics included. And some topics were included because they are thought provoking and raise provocative questions that may help readers improve their crit-ical reasoning skills, which are essential to all ethical inquiry.

Finally, this book takes a clear stand on certain issues such as mas-turbation (that it is not wrong) and nonmarital sex (that it is not *al-ways* wrong), which you, the reader, should feel free to oppose. (But on one issue there can be no debate: any type of sexual behavior that involves force, coercion, or abuse of any sort is unacceptable—no matter what the circumstances.)

Explaining the difference between finding moral truth and the tol-erance of moral viewpoints that differ from your own is very difficult, and beyond the scope of this book. If, however, after reading this book, you are clearer about some principle, such as the necessity for consent in sex, and more understanding (and perhaps, more tolerant) toward people whose moral standards differ from your own, then you will be several leagues ahead in the quest for sexual morality.

SEX. SEX. SEX.

Today, talk show guests reveal the most intimate details of their sexual lives, while many schools offer frank curricula that might have made sexuality pioneers such as Sigmund Freud and Havelock Ellis blush. Sex scandals rock politicians from their roosts, and explicit sex scenes entertain millions of movie fans. In fact, few can escape the general barrage of sexual messages hurled at them by the media or society.

Sex. Sex. Sex. It occurs most often among the married or cohabiting (people who live together without being married)—on the average of six to seven times a month.[3] Today, the average American male will have at least six partners in his lifetime, and the average female will have two sexual partners in her lifetime.[4] And some Americans surpass those averages in just a year.

By the time they are thirty years old, the majority of Americans are married or living with someone with whom they are having a satisfying sexual life.[5]

Many people divorce, remarry, or acquire a new sexual partner at the end of their marriage. During the marriage, however, Americans usually remain monogamous. Still, one out of every five to ten spouses will have an extramarital affair before age sixty-five.[6] Many Americans, especially those who are are involved in satisfying sexual relationships, have sex with themselves.[7] Some have sex with persons of their own gender.[8] And a rare few change their gender altogether.

11

Quite an alarming number of people depart from any moral path and either initiate sex with children or force themselves on people who don't want to have sex with them, causing untold harm and distress.[9]

Some Americans have more than one partner at a time. A few are having sex with people they hardly know or with people they do not know and are never going to see again.[10] And Americans are having sex in conventional and unconventional ways.

Despite the fact that it is illegal in most states to pay to have sex, or to offer sex for money, there are those who do. And when they aren't sexually active, many people actively seek sex—sometimes any way they can: Harassment. Voyeurism. Pornography. Indeed, the sexual landscape in the United States, while for the most part conventional, displays great diversity.

THE YOUNG AND THE RESTLESS

No matter how much the media and arts paint a picture of a hotbed of sexual activity in America, one of the most recent surveys, described in the book *Sex in America,* reveals that most Americans lead rather conventional sex lives.[11] Clearly not *everyone* is "doing it,"— particularly not young teenagers.

Nor should sexuality be viewed so narrowly, for it encompasses an exceedingly wide range of activity. Most people love kissing, touching, and hugging.[12] Even a simple gaze can spark a sexual charge between two people who are strongly attracted to each other. Sexual intimacy can be achieved without having intercourse. Nevertheless, a substantial number of teenagers (especially compared to previous generations) are having sexual intercourse, although many are having it somewhat infrequently. A 1994 study of high school students[13] produced this profile:

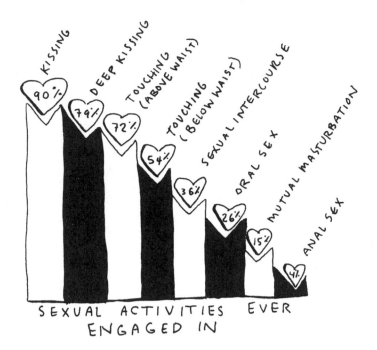

KISSING 90%
DEEP KISSING 79%
TOUCHING (ABOVE WAIST) 72%
TOUCHING (BELOW WAIST) 54%
SEXUAL INTERCOURSE 36%
ORAL SEX 26%
MUTUAL MASTURBATION 15%
ANAL SEX 4%

SEXUAL ACTIVITIES EVER
ENGAGED IN

By graduation, 55 percent of the students had experienced intercourse at least once.[14]

Despite a widespread concern about contracting sexually transmitted disease, despite access to birth control and disease prevention, despite sex education programs that urge teens to remain chaste or to act responsibly, a startling number of teenagers routinely take risks.[15] Many also suffer the consequences of such risk-taking behavior.

According to the U.S. Department of Health, one in every twenty-five high school students contracts a sexually transmitted disease.[16] And each year, a million teenage women—one in every nine female teenagers—will become pregnant.[17]

Statistics like these can be mind-boggling or too abstract to personalize. They are also general findings. For example, while the "average" teen has sexual intercourse at age sixteen,[18] many teens acquire a great deal of sexual experience without ever having had intercourse. And many teens postpone having sexual intercourse until after high school. Furthermore, among some high school populations, the vast majority of students have experienced sexual intercourse by the time they graduate from high school, and many of them are already parents. In other school populations, especially among students who earn good grades and look forward to furthering their education, sexual experience and teen parenthood are less common. Finally, statistics fail to explain why one in ten teens has never experienced any kind of sexual contact with another person at all.[19]

Nor do some teenagers seem to be scared by the numbers concerning disease and pregnancy. Instead, they choose to ignore them by saying, "It won't happen to me." And the lucky ones may even beat the odds.

Failure to beat the odds requires dealing with the consequences—in a 100 percent manner. There is no such thing as a "partial" pregnancy or "half an STD." Either you are or you aren't. Either you have a sexually transmitted disease or you don't. If so, life may never be headed on the same course again. Just one unprotected act of sex with someone infected with gonorrhea gives a woman a great chance (2 to 1) of contracting gonorrhea. And gonorrhea is one of the leading causes of ectopic pregnancy (a life-threatening situation in which the embryo grows outside the uterus), infertility (inability to conceive), and persistent pelvic pain later in life.[20]

Moreover, while statistics paint an interesting picture of the young and restless (and to many parents and educators, an increasingly alarming picture), they hardly constitute an accurate moral guidepost: *moral behavior does not depend on numbers; it depends on moral principles.*

No matter how many or how few teenagers engage in a particular sexual custom, their numbers alone do not render a custom moral or immoral—only principles do that. For example, it may be customary and common to sexually harass girls at school, but such conduct is never right. Conversely, although relatively few people date someone of a different race,[21] that alone does not make a particular relationship immoral.

MINDFUL CHOICES

Many people take a practical view of sexuality. They say no to sexual intercourse and thereby avoid any of its risks or negative consequences.

Others choose to have sexual intercourse but, again, take a practical approach to it. They recognize the risks, and at the same time recognize the need to act responsibly. Appreciating the satisfaction they derive from sex, these people try to minimize the risks but acknowledge the ones that remain.

Others refuse to worry or restrain their sexual conduct at all, preferring instead to gamble on the odds, and facing the situations that later arise.

Still others rationalize their sexual behavior. Some people, for instance, rely on sex to win popularity or acceptance and, perhaps, the love and affection denied them as children, ignoring the fact that sex alone cannot provide emotional security.

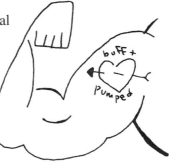

We can add another perspective to our sexual behavior, however, in addition to considerations of practical-

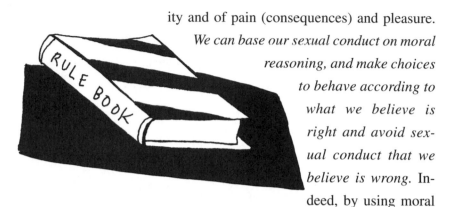

ity and of pain (consequences) and pleasure. *We can base our sexual conduct on moral reasoning, and make choices to behave according to what we believe is right and avoid sexual conduct that we believe is wrong.* Indeed, by using moral standards to guide our sexual behavior, we improve our general character. And when our sexual conduct is based on conscious moral choices, when these are morally good choices, then we can experience a richness and emotional depth unattainable through any other mindset. At the same time, we minimize the pain that an unexamined sexual morality could cause ourselves or others.

Many parents, educators, and religious leaders try to tell teenagers how to act, and what to do and not do sexually. Moral living requires both the freedom and the ability to choose behavior on your own terms, though. It also requires wisdom, sensitivity to others, and restraint.

When you read this book, you may or may not be sexually experienced. No matter, there is something for everyone here—except an exclusive moral code! All discussions are centered on the idea that it is good to be kind, tolerant, and fair toward others, and that the search for moral truth leads to right answers more often than to wrong ones (though some critics may debate this). Read this book to help you sort through the sexual issues you face now, or may face later, as well as a few that you might have overlooked or ignored. Finally, use it to help you think more clearly, to think twice before you act, and to learn to be a sexually responsible person.

IN THE COURSE OF HISTORY

It is easy to claim that because we live in a free society, we are free to behave any way we want. But societies have a way of imposing rules on their members. Some of these rules are written as laws. Others are enforced informally, through the guilt, shame, or discomfort we feel after breaking the rules. For example, we have no laws about dating someone of a different religion or social class. Yet in some families, doing so elicits such strong disapproval, perhaps even total rejection, that someone may be "free" to break the rule but unwilling to do so because of the consequences they will encounter.

In order to appreciate and understand the sexual morality of our society today, it helps to know how we arrived here and why our ideas about sexual morality are so diverse. We can do that by taking a look at the history of sexual ethics.

Summing up the entire history of sexual ethics, one young man explained, "I guess sex was originally to produce another body; then I guess it was for love; nowadays it's just for feeling good."[1] He left it to philosophers to explain why!

The ancient Hebrews, who came up with some of the first rules of morality for sexuality, perceived the issue as this: Make babies; make sure you know whose babies you are making; and (for women at least) don't stray from home to make them. A pretty clear recipe.

In contrast to Hebrew law, pagan worship encouraged nonmarital sex. Temple prostitutes served the gods by sexually serving the men who attended temple. And in ancient Rome and Greece alike, though marital sex was the norm, both prostitution and homosexual sex were acceptable.

Classical Greek philosophers, in particular Plato, expounded on the subject of sexual ethics. Plato took a restrained view. Reasoning that body-and-sexuality have no connection to mind-and-reason, he concluded that mindful contemplation of life and love without sex (now called Platonic love) is superior to erotic love (with sex).

Later, two monks, Augustine and Aquinas, born nearly a thousand years apart, shaped the sexual ethic of Roman Catholicism. Augustine (A.D. 344–430), drawing on both a cultural and religious heritage, taught that when Adam and Eve disobeyed instructions and ate of the Tree of Knowledge, the danger, uncontrollability, and sinfulness of sex were released for all humans to follow. As a result, devout Catholics believe that sex must be controlled, either through celibacy (no sex at all) or by restricting it to marriage.

Taking a cue from the work of Aristotle, medieval monk Thomas Aquinas developed a rational theory of sexuality, which he based on what he called "natural law"—natural to animals and humans. Because he was a deeply pious man, Aquinas illuminated his natural law with Divine Revelation and the will of God.

From his observations of animals, Aquinas could detect no masturbation (some animals do masturbate, but Aquinas never observed those species). Therefore, he concluded, masturbation is unnatural and, thus, immoral. In fact, people who follow Aquinas consider anything that interferes with the "normal sexual act" as unnatural and sinful. This constraint covers oral sex, anal sex, sex between homosexuals, and all practices that interfere with the ability of a man's sperm to impregnate his sexual partner (birth control, such as the condom, an IUD, or diaphragm, for example).

According to Aquinas, parents should provide whatever is required to rear any offspring they do have. Both sex and childrearing, he taught, are moral only in the context of marriage. Finally, observing the roles of animals during sex (males acting as aggressors to receptive females), Aquinas also decided that it is natural (and therefore good) for men to govern women.[2] This "Thomastic" concept of sexual morality wielded a strong influence on Western culture, and continues to be the Vatican's official position on sexual conduct.[3]

Jewish and Protestant views on sexuality took separate courses. While Jewish scholars also emphasized the importance of pregnancy and the control of bodily passion, they interpreted the story of Adam and Eve quite differently than did Augustine and Aquinas. According to David Biale, author of an historic account of Jewish sexual ethics, *Eros and the Jews,* the rabbis believed that the fall of Adam and Eve was punishment for their disobeying God, and not for the discovery of sexuality itself.[4]

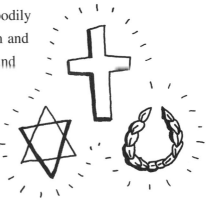

Furthermore, although humans act with a tendency toward sexual abandon at times, rabbinical thought stresses that sexual moderation and modesty can control such lack of restraint.

In Judaism, it is a commandment from God and a blessing for all Jewish men to marry and have children. At the same time, every Jewish woman has a right to receive sexual pleasure from her husband, even when she is pregnant, or if she is postmenopausal, or infertile (unable to conceive a child or carry a pregnancy to term). However, masturbation and having sex with a menstruating partner or while menstruating are violations of Orthodox Jewish law.

During the Enlightenment, new Christian denominations, under the general umbrella of Protestantism, were formed outside the sphere of the Vatican. Some of these new churches retained Augustine's theory of original sin, but most of them chose to reinterpret biblical text. These theological discussions and debates produced fresh ideas about sexual morality.

As in Jewish sexual ethics, Protestant scholarship teaches that the purpose of sex is not only to create new life but to bond a husband and wife together emotionally and spiritually. Consequently, sex for pleasure—within the context of marriage—helps to sanctify the holy state of matrimony and enable "the two to become one flesh."

In the eighteenth century, the French and American Revolutions, with their emphasis on basic human rights, led to changes in moral reasoning about sexual conduct. Still later, various philosophers, politicians, feminists, and humanists heralded the concept of women's equality in marriage and sex. Others stressed the idea of eroticism and pleasure in sexuality. With a focus on sexual freedom and sexual gratification, however, their ideas remained out of sync with the general sexual ethics of the society until well into the twentieth century.[5]

CUPID IN THE BEDROOM

One of the most significant influences on sexual ethics, besides traditional philosophy and religious teachings, is the idea of romantic love,[6] a universal notion found in nearly all cultures.[7] In the West, romantic love was glorified by stories about the nobility in Europe during the Middle Ages, when knights and troubadours were allowed to "court" and love a married woman. Yet, although a knight in shining armor was permitted to tuck "his lady" into bed at nightfall, he was expected to leave her chaste—according to some interpreters.[8]

Over the next several hundred years, this notion of sexual purity in romantic love evolved into one of sex-for-love. In time, single men were expected to pursue unmarried maidens so that when they found their true love, the two could marry and spend their lives together, loving one another. The quest for true love appealed to all social classes and inspired nearly everyone to wholeheartedly embrace the notion of romantic love.[9]

In contemporary times, Cupid, god of love, was found romping with Eros, god of sexuality. Americans now had unchaperoned dating and the automobile (with the privacy these provided), as well as improved birth control. Together, these new freedoms lured many people into premarital sexual relationships and extramarital trysts. Our sexual standards and sexual conduct underwent radical changes, and orthodox religion's grip on the sexual behavior of many people was loosened.[10] Nearly everyone in the United States was marrying for love; and by the 1960s, falling *out* of love became a legal and moral justification for scrambling out of a marriage.

SEXUAL REVOLUTION

In the mid-1800s, physicians began to place the blame for certain disorders such as hysteria and depression on sex,[11] especially on masturbation. Theories ranged from the belief that too much sex caused a disorder to the idea that repressing sexuality is bad. Dr. John Harvey Kellogg, inventor of Kellogg's Corn Flakes, believed that a healthful diet could inhibit people from masturbating and help them control their sexual desires. This, in turn, would ensure better health. Sylvester Graham, inventor of the graham cracker, also advised against masturbation, which he suggested could transform a young boy into a "confirmed and degraded idiot."[12]

Later in that century, a wave of scientific inventions included the invention of vulcanized rubber, which was used for mass-produced condoms and diaphragms. This ushered in an intense interest in population and birth control.

By the turn of the century, Sigmund Freud, father of modern psychology, was espousing novel theories on childhood sexuality and the nature of our sexual drive. A few decades later, Havelock Ellis, a biologist, researched and published volumes on the biology of human sexuality and human reproduction, incorporating his very liberal viewpoints on sexual ethics.

In 1948 and 1953, Alfred Kinsey issued two landmark reports on the sexual behavior of American men and women respectively. They documented an enormous gap between our sexual ideals and what we thought other people did or didn't do, and what their sexual behavior actually was. Although Kinsey failed to use a scientifically accurate sample, his published findings caused a sensation. For the first time, the American public learned that substantial numbers of them masturbated regularly, had premarital coitus, committed adultery, experienced homosexual sex, and engaged in heavy petting.[13] And many

22

people reckoned that if so many others were behaving this way, maybe their behavor wasn't so abnormal or immoral after all.

The National Organization of Women (NOW), founded in 1965, heralded a second wave of feminism, and with it, a quest for sexual freedom. In 1969 a riot at the Stonewall bar in New York City, where the struggle for gay rights began, marshaled many activists to a new quest for equality and sexual freedom.

By 1973, Americans had reliable birth control, antibiotics to cure syphilis and gonorrhea, and access to legal abortions. These factors, along with a general air of social rebellion—stemming in part from cynicism over the Vietnam War and from the sixties' commitment to create a freer, more just society—ushered in a period of the most liberal sexual standards of any in our history, particularly among college students. Not long afterward, scholars and moralists followed with an unprecedented interest in sexual ethics.

The old stereotypes and myths were rapidly replaced by new ones. Sex and the single girl. The New Age man. Swinging singles. The joy of sex. Albert Ellis's book *Sex Without Guilt* and Bertrand Russell's classic essay on trial marriage served as scripts for "sexually liberated" men and women. American society entered an intense period of self-analysis, sexual experimentation, and exploration as people searched for personal fulfillment. Through therapy and group encounters, men supposedly got more in touch with their feelings and women learned to free themselves of sexism.

Masters and Johnson pioneered sexual research in the laboratory, documenting for the first time in scientific history the nature of erections and orgasms. This research spawned a new field—sexual therapy—and many people clamored for help with their sexual performances and enjoyment.

Actually, individuals and groups had broken sexual taboos and trespassed on forbidden moral ground before this modern age. Back in the 1840s, for example, Mormons were practicing polygamy (having more than one wife), and members of the Oneida community, in New York State, were practicing free love (casual sex with many partners).[14] The difference is that these groups were on the *fringe* of society and not in its mainstream. Yet, according to sociologist Ira Reiss of the University of Minnesota, by the 1960s mainstream Americans were also breaking the taboos. Reiss states that as early as the 1920s, half of all women and four-fifths of all men in America were breaking the societal "rule" against premarital sex.[15]

By the time of the Sexual Revolution, as the new era in sexual norms was dubbed, unprecedented numbers of people, including young adults and adult singles, ignored the traditional barriers— boldly, relentlessly, and apparently without too much guilt, shame, remorse, or fear. Some were tearing them down altogether, with an unabashed level of promiscuity, especially in the new gay neighborhoods clustered in cities such as San Francisco and New York.[16]

The number of people openly engaging in premarital, nonmarital, and extramarital sex soared, and the number of people cohabitating skyrocketed. Divorce rates increased, and the number of both abortions and teenage pregnancies rose dramatically, too.[17]

Perhaps the biggest contributor to the new sexual ethical terrain, however, was change itself. As soon as people heard the message that "everyone is doing it," many felt justified doing it themselves. And a few people tried doing it all. Group sex, sex with strangers, and sex using toys. Yoko Ono and John Lennon bared their bodies on a record album cover; campus streakers bared their all, with little restraint or concern for authority. "Mooning" was in, and prudery was out.

With college curfews and dorm restrictions gone, sex became a vital part of campus social life. Even the guru of child rearing during the baby boom years, septuagenarian Dr. Benjamin Spock, flaunted convention by divorcing his wife of thirty years to marry his thirty-something nurse. In fact, Spock took much of the flak for the wave of permissiveness sweeping society.

Certainly, not everyone participated in the Sexual Revolution, particularly not those who were middle-aged or older. Many people still played by the old rules—but they no longer dominated the playing field. Nor did everyone consider the new atmosphere social progress. As Lillian Rubin, author of *The Erotic Wars*, observes, "The [sexual] revolution, which had freed women to say yes, also disabled them from saying no."[18]

By the time AIDS was discovered, about 1981, the Sexual Revolution was in high gear, at least among certain groups in America. And today, despite the relative conservativism of most people's sexual behavior, the rules about what is acceptable and what isn't show few signs that the clock of history is going to be rewound.[19]

CHOOSING FROM THE MORAL MENU

The study of ethics requires that we search for a moral compass to guide our behavior and help us choose right from wrong and good from bad. In sexual ethics, this means finding sexual standards that help us behave in a good way. Yet American society is diverse, a diversity we call "pluralism," and people and groups within our society have different sexual standards.

Even though Americans have a tendency to choose sexual partners with backgrounds similar to their own,[1] they are likely, at least on some occasions, to become involved with people whose ideas differ. Too, the likelihood of having friends and aquaintances with divergent sexual standards increases as people expand their social circles at school, on vacations, and through the workplace.

Some of these sexual standards are conservative and come from religious ideas about sexual morality. Others are exceedingly liberal. While people with a liberal sexual standard may also be religious or spiritual, about half of them are not.[2]

We can use philosophical reasoning to evaluate these various sexual standards and determine right conduct. Most people, however, don't function that way, and rarely apply such rational reasoning to their behavior (though perhaps they should!). Instead, they accept the moral rules and guidelines of their parents, religious groups, peers, and even the media, and modify these rules through personal experiences.

Because human behavior and, in particular, sexual behavior, is so complex, it is difficult to describe every view of sexual morality in America. Still, for the sake of discussion, the various moral standards will be grouped under a number of "moral compasses" (sets of rules that determine how a person is going to behave and what he or she believes is right or wrong).

A RELIGIOUS IDEAL

In God We Trust

The most conservative moral standards are rooted in religious traditions, namely the belief that sex is a blessing intended by God, within the context of marriage. Here, sex is considered morally good, but only if it is channeled into responsible behavior.[3] For most orthodox religious denominations, responsible behavior means heterosexual, foreplay and vaginal intercourse, either for the purpose of having children or to enhance the marital bond. It excludes certain behavior that is considered "deviant" from this standard, such as homosexuality or anal sex. And for the most traditional denominations, such as

Roman Catholicism and Orthodox Judaism, it excludes masturbation as well.

Within such viewpoints, sexual virginity for both bride and groom is a virtue; fidelity afterward an obligation. The essential purpose of sex is to produce children, though for certain religions, sexual relations are also used to forge a spiritual and emotional bond, a union that combines two personalities into a singular expression of selfless, married love.

Not all theologians interpret religious law so strictly. Instead, with a more liberal outlook that acknowledges a person's right to sexual gratification and the loving, pleasurable purpose of sex, they allow modern methods of birth control and fertilization, abortion in certain circumstances, such as rape, and a variety of sexual behavior that includes oral sex and masturbation.[4]

Because of the restraints placed on sexuality in certain religions, sex and sin are strongly associated with each other. This can cause tremendous guilt in anyone who fails to live up to this particular moral code. Moreover, people with these beliefs who marry late and have repressed their sexual urges for many years may experience difficulty overcoming their inhibitions and guilt when they finally do engage in sexual intimacy.

Some denominations prohibit the use of reliable birth control. This can cause a great deal of anxiety and worry about pregnancy, and can squelch sexual ardor, even within marriage. Finally, unless a person dates only those sharing similar standards and traditions, with strict chaperoning, sticking to these standards represents a formidable challenge today.

On the other hand, there are rich rewards for a conscience guided by traditional religious principles. These include moral certainty, because there is little confusion or dispute about what is acceptable sexual conduct.[5] Saving sexual intimacy for marriage protects partners from feeling jealous about past sexual relationships. And with this moral compass to guide them, people avoid exposure to sexually transmitted disease, sexual scandal, and the like. According to Orthodox rabbi Mani Friedman, author of *Doesn't Anyone Blush Anymore?*, conservative sexual behavior preserves and strengthens the marital bond between two people.[6]

Although a few of those who subscribe to this compass do so for nonreligious reasons, most trust in God's law as the *only* morally decent way to live.

BOYS WILL BE BOYS
The Double Standard

This next moral compass differs from the previous religious one in an important way: here, what's good for the fellows is not necessarily good for the women. The basis for such reasoning is that the differences between men and women supposedly require a different set of rules for each. Basically, men are permitted to be more sexually active, assertive, and adventuresome than women. Historically, such a perspective was called "the double standard" (though critics call it, simply, hypocrisy).

According to the double standard, a woman is expected to be a virgin when she marries—or at least when she becomes engaged to be married. In contrast, men are allowed, and even encouraged, to acquire sexual experience before marriage. Also, a few men believe that after marriage it is all right to "have a little on the side" by visiting prostitutes, having an extramarital affair, or by maintaining a mistress.

Rationalizations for the double standard are based on two ideas: First, by requiring a woman's faithfulness, the husband knows with certainty that any offspring in their marriage are his and entitled to his support and inheritance. In times when only the children of legitimate marriages could inherit from their fathers, this was an important consideration. Second, the double standard promotes the idea, whether true or false, that men need to and can live by a freer set of rules. "Boys will be boys," after all.

Sociologist Ira Reiss believes that such reasoning is often based on erroneous assumptions that men cannot repress their sexual urges without dire consequences, and that women have a lesser sex drive than do men.[7] According to author and feminist Naomi Wolf, the need to explode these myths (that women have less of a sex drive or that they are entitled to less sexual fulfillment) is the crux of feminism, and of society's uneasiness with it. "The basic principle of social organization," explains Wolf, "is not just who gets power, but who gets pleasure."[8]

There are other problems with the double standard. It encourages men to exploit women and use them solely for their own gratification. Once a man has "scored," he may show little care for the woman with whom he has just had sex. These men also have a tendency to dismiss any woman who is easily lured into a sexual relationship. Similarly, men may ignore or even contribute to the many social, economic, or emotional reasons that lead women to have sex with these men or to have sex with so many partners.

Besides exploiting women, the double standard also encourages a self-centered sexuality that frequently is devoid of commitment and affection. Further, this kind of sexual behavior hardly prepares men for the give-and-take that an emotionally rich, satisfying sexual relationship requires.

Living under a double standard has adverse effects on women, too. Those women who are comfortable with their sexuality and choose an active sexual life may earn reputations for being "easy," and get saddled with labels such as "fast," "whore," and "slut." To avoid a bad reputation and maintain their desirability as wives, women may hide their true desires to initiate sex, instead becoming sexual teases. And when they are restricted to sending only subtle clues about their sexual desires, women may send out unclear signals, which men can easily misread.

Other women feign sexual innocence, lying to their sexual partners about any sexual experiences. In the past especially, putting up such facades often required the painful harboring of secrets about infants given up for adoption, abortions, and sexual abuse or assault.

Finally, treating women as inferior, as the double sexual standard does, encourages their devaluation in the rest of society—be it the workplace, school, home, or anywhere else. Worse, as Reiss points out in both *Journey Into Sexuality* and *An End to Shame,* by holding women to an inferior status while simultaneously encouraging men to treat sex as a conquest over women, the double standard "can actually contribute to the cause of rape."[9]

EMOTIONAL BONDING

Instead of turning to a strict religious code for moral guidance, many people turn to secular (nonreligious) moral principles to help them determine right from wrong. Or they belong to religious denominations, such as Reform Judaism, that hold somewhat liberal views of sexual behavior compared with the more conservative religious views previously discussed. This moral compass, undoubtedly one of the most popular,[10] sanctions sex outside of marriage, but only where two people have mutual respect, love, or affection for one another.

According to the sexual standards in this moral compass, sexual intimacy strengthens a couple's relationship and satisfies both their physical and emotional needs. Furthermore, men and women are considered to have equal sexual rights and responsibilities. Thus, while sexual intimacy does not require a wedding vow, or even, perhaps, a long-term commitment to the relationship, people *are* expected to have affection for their sexual partners, and to make an emotional investment in the relationship.

How much emotional commitment a relationship requires varies. Some people believe that two people should have a solid, long-term commitment to each other before they engage in any sexually intimate behavior. This may be an intention of marriage or, at the very least, being in love. At the more liberal end of the spectrum, however, are those who believe that sex does not require a long-term commitment, only a mutual respect between partners.

This is a broad standard that encompasses a wide range of thought on monogamy and fidelity. Most people believe that all sexual relationships should be monogamous, if only for practical reasons such

as protection from sexually transmitted disease. Some, though, believe that as long as there is affection, openness, and mutual consent, then secondary sexual relationships are acceptable.

With this moral compass, most people put less emphasis on sexual coitus (intercourse) and more on the entire context of sexuality and feelings. Furthermore, rather than limit sexual behavior in a strict manner, they interpret it loosely, following traditional ethical principles for making decisions about their sexual behavior: Do not harm, exploit, use, or deceive another person before, during, or after sexual encounters. Thus, especially among the more liberal-minded, as long as you abide by these basic principles, most kinds of sexual behavior between two consenting people are acceptable.

Advocates of this liberal standard argue that it is the healthiest emotional preparation for marriage and the best way to live an unmarried life. On the other hand, unless people take precautions (and even then), they risk getting a sexually transmitted disease or having to deal with pregnancy outside of marriage. And some people who profess to live by this compass don't really understand it. As a familiar adage says: "Women give sex for love and men give love for sex."

NO STRINGS ATTACHED

According to this last moral compass, sex has broad appeal—not only for the opportunity it offers for emotionally bonding to another person, but for the physical pleasure, or at least a fleeting intimacy between two people who have little commitment to a future together. Reiss calls this standard "permissiveness without affection," because sex here involves no emotional commitment. It is sex without affection.

A few people in this crowd will have sex with anyone—free love, orgies, one-night stands, and anonymous pickups that offer sexual freedom to the max. Although some advocates of this extremely liberal compass impose occasional limits on their sexual behavior, many are somewhat nonconforming, adventuresome, and occasionally reckless about sex. Ranging from casual, or recreational, sex between two partners unready or unwilling to make an emotional commitment to totally anonymous sex among multiple strangers, this compass covers 360 degrees of sexual freedom.

Good sex. No strings attached. Whatever turns you on. Devoid of emotion or commitment, can such sex really be "good"?

While advocates may still uphold such moral principles as refraining from harm, deceit, or coercion, the seemingly total freedom of this compass may lead them to occasionally ignore these principles. Flight from responsibility, cynicism about relationships, and burnout over sex are other pitfalls. So is an empty or degenerate feeling that may follow from having sex with a partner who cares little or nothing about you afterward, or from sex that is degrading or painful. And children conceived during such casual or anonymous encounters hardly have the same emotional advantages as those born within a loving family.

In addition to the emotional risks, sex with strangers carries the risk of abuse or assault. That a sexual encounter can be dangerous, though, is its very appeal to some people. Even the threat of dying cannot scare them into abandoning their sexually free, no-strings-attached lifestyle.

For some people, purely recreational sex is a temporary choice. While they are *willing* to settle for sex without affection, they would *prefer* a more emotionally gratifying relationship. Or, exercising their own double standard, some people withhold affection from certain partners and even sexually exploit them, but lavish it on others.

Some critics of this moral compass claim that it has no morality at all—that by treating sex as only a physical and not an emotional act, they place sex in the same category as "eating a good meal, listening to music, or getting a pleasant back rub."[11] This perspective short-changes them of the moral richness that can be derived from sex. Conversely, proponents of the no-strings-attached code believe that by isolating physical sex from emotions, people can be more honest in their relationships, thereby avoiding the game playing and deception that can occur with other sexual standards, particularly the double standard. And for many, sex without affection or commitment seems better than no sex at all.

IN TUNE WITH YOUR CONSCIENCE

"Be true to yourself and stick by your own moral standards" is a constant theme in moral education. Yet sex nearly always involves at least two people, who may have different sexual moral standards. How can we be tolerant of a moral viewpoint different from our own? If people whose respect we want put pressure on us, how can we maintain our own standards? Most of all, how can we make wise, informed choices about our sexual conduct?

"Selling out" on your sexual standards can cause not only shame and guilt but also regret. Dr. Pam Brubocker, a professor of sexual ethics at Cleveland State University, observes that students who profess the most regrets about their sexual past are the ones who lowered their standards to accommodate themselves to someone else's expectations.[12]

Besides exposing your sexual standards to a thorough philosophical analysis, Brubocker suggests the "mirror approach": If you do what you decide is right to do, can you still look yourself in the mirror and have respect for yourself?

"Do the right thing." But how does a person determine what is *truly* right sexual behavior? (It is the question all sexual ethicists and moralists ask.) Reiss, following Brubocker, offers another litmus test, one that takes into account the fact that different people have different moral standards. It also considers the fact that people have freedom of choice over their behavior, a choice he suggests tempering with moral restraint. "It's not a question of just say 'yes' or just say 'no,'" says Reiss, but rather one of choosing wisely—and respecting the choices that other people make. "If we oppose the prohibition of alcohol, that does not mean we favor drunkenness," explains Reiss. "A person can be sexually tolerant [of other people's standards] and still be discriminating [about their own sexual conduct]."[13] In other words, live and let live.

Developing your own moral judgment is difficult. "It takes careful self-examination and patience to work out one's own preferred sexual lifestyle."[14] And much of this moral development occurs by learning from experience, including the mistakes.

Finally, Reiss suggests that no matter what sexual behavior you choose for yourself, it should always be based on a concern for the well-being of both others and yourself. This is possible only if "all sexual encounters are negotiated with an honest statement of your feelings, an equal recognition of the other person's feelings, and taking a responsibility for avoiding unwanted outcomes like pregnancy or disease."[15]

Choosing from the moral menu does not mean taking the easiest pathway—though indeed the one you follow may prove to be simple and practical; nor is it as straightforward as selecting one you decide is best for you. Instead, choose what you believe is the *right* way to behave sexually. Other people with a vested interest in the way you behave, especially your immediate family, may try to persuade you that their way is the right way—and perhaps it is. Even so, it is important to examine those sexual standards before making them your own.

Many people, in the quest for tolerance, want to believe that all four of these moral compasses can be truthful and right, even though they represent very different claims. The belief that each one is right is called moral relativism. And moral relativism offers very little in the way of moral certainty or truth. It is much like navigating with a compass whose four sides all read North. On the other hand, as women and children have gained rights, including the right to be free of sexual oppression; as gays still struggle for their rights; as casual sex for some becomes a dance with death; we can learn that among these various compasses there is moral truth. Exactly what that truth is, ethical inquiry and experience can reveal.

4

ASK FIRST

Zach planned a romantic prom weekend with Jill—dinner in a cozy restaurant, moonlight drive to the beach after the prom, and a few bottles of wine. Although they had dated for a long time, Jill had never consented to have sexual intercourse with Zach. "I'm not ready yet," she told him, reasoning that she didn't want to risk getting pregnant and ruining her chance of going away to college.

"Please . . . for me," Zach pleaded with Jill. "You know I love you."

"Seduced" by the romance of the evening, however, and woozy from all the wine they drank, that night Jill had intercourse with Zach.

Ill-prepared for the evening's turn of events, Jill failed to use birth control (as did Zach, also). Furthermore, she was disappointed with both Zach and herself. Even though it turned out to be a romantically charged experience, Jill had not really wanted to have sexual intercourse *then*, especially without protection. But Zach had

been so persistent, giving her his old line that if she loved
him, she would want to go all the way with him. Sure, Jill
wanted to—Zach was correct about that. But it didn't feel
right to her, at least not yet. Why couldn't Zach take no
for an answer and still keep loving her?

The other question that kept churning in Jill's mind
was whether or not it was fair of her to put the entire
blame on Zach, since he hadn't *forced* her to drink the
wine or have intercourse. After all, did she have to say
yes when she meant no?

With all these issues to consider, Jill couldn't decide if the incident happened because she lacked willpower, or if Zach was to blame
for unfairly persuading or coercing her.

IN THE DRIVER'S SEAT

Morality requires an ability to think clearly and the freedom to choose
between right and wrong. In sexual ethics, such reasoning and freedom are the factors that constitute an essential issue—consent. Consent means the obligation to *ask for,* and not *demand,* sex—and the
willingness to accept no for an answer. It also requires that you be true
to yourself when you decide whether or not to consent to any sexual
behavior.

Even people with the most liberal viewpoints recognize that coercing others into having any kind of sex against their will is always
wrong, because it denies them freedom over their own moral behavior. (Interestingly, such coercion also removes any moral responsibility for what occurs. Hence, a person who has been date raped
cannot be *morally* blamed for the incident.)

Yet despite the immorality of coercion, many women (and some men) have been forced to do something sexual against their will.[1] For younger women, the news is even more disturbing. At least 3 out of 4 of all young females who have had sexual intercourse before the age of 14 were coerced.[2] And at least 7 percent of all sexually experienced young people ages 18 to 22 have been forced to engage in some sexual behavior against their will at least once.[3]

Even when coercion is absent, subtle pressure can still erode a person's freedom to choose. A school celebrity, such as a star quarterback, may use his status to convince someone who is insecure and seeking the security of a relationship to have sex. Or, someone can threaten to withdraw affection if a partner refuses to have sexual intercourse or perform a disagreeable sexual act.

On the other hand, what responsibility did Jill have to stay sober enough to keep a clear head and maintain her self-control in the situation? After all, most reported cases of date rape occur when alcohol or drugs are being used by either the assailant or the victim.[4] Furthermore, when drunk, many young people abandon the precautions they would take if sober. Most students who have acquired a sexually transmitted disease—at least 60 percent, according to one study—were under the influence of alcohol at the time they had intercourse.[5] There is little mystery to this, since binge drinkers (those who have four to five drinks in a row) are seven times more likely to have unprotected sex.[6]

In an ideal world, we could trust everyone to respect our sexual rights. As long as society has members who fall short of the ideal, though, everyone must assume full responsibility for themselves. That may mean avoiding situations where forced sex is more likely to occur. It also means not giving away the right to choose by getting too drunk to resist sex or to give informed consent (informed consent is when you are fully aware of what you are choosing to do).

In the largest study of its kind, Mary P. Koss, Ph.D., then a professor at Kent State University, found that:

- 1 in 4 women will be a victim of rape or attempted rape
- 15 percent of all female students had experienced forced sex
- another 12 percent had to resist unwanted sex[7]

Even though so many women are victims of rape or attempted rape, Dr. Koss also found that most of the female students failed to perceive that sex has been wrongly forced on them. And although the majority of men (90 percent) had admitted to forcing sex on a woman at some time, most of them failed to understand that forcing sex on a person is wrong.[8] Nor are such misunderstandings between the sexes limited to college campuses. The University of Chicago sex survey, conducted in 1994, found the same high rate of coercion and miscommunication.[9]

If women fail to realize that being forced to have sex is wrong, and men fail to understand that they are wrong for forcing a woman to have sex, what *is* everyone thinking?

Actually, many people perceive coercive sex as a normal part of a relationship. In fact, some female students blame themselves for being forced to have sex. In contrast, the male offenders often stated that the women they had pressured into having sex had been ambivalent about wanting sex. Or else, the women *had* tried to convey that they didn't want sex, but the men had misread their cues as signals to continue the pressure. The line of demarcation between consent and regret, however blurred, is essential. As one male student mused, "As far as I'm concerned, you can change your mind before, even during, but just not *after* sex."[10]

Even now, after widespread publicity and education about the issue of date rape, many young women continue to tolerate unwanted sexual advances, and many young men fail to understand that such behavior is wrong. One nationwide survey of high school and junior high school students released in 1993 found that most students (87 percent of the girls and 76 percent of the boys in grades 8 through 11) were subjected to unwelcome sexual behavior at least once in their school lives. In a different study, two-thirds of the girls reported being harassed often or occasionally.[11]

Just as surprisingly, in still another survey, conducted in 1993 by *Seventeen* magazine, 2 out of every 5 students reported being harassed *every single school day*.[12] Moreover, quite a number of students believe that such behavior is "just a part of school life" and "no big deal."[13]

In his book *An End to Shame*, sociologist Ira L. Reiss says that much of the fault for miscommunication over sex, as well as the high incidence of date rape, lies in our society's traditional script for dating, one that casts women in the "sexually reluctant" role and men in the role of "persuader." This kind of scripting works against honest communication. Many women give unclear cues about their sexual desires, and many (or, as the surveys suggest, most) men misconstrue them. "Both men and women must stop playing this dangerous sexual guessing game," advises Reiss, "and sit down and tell each other how they feel about the relationship and about having sex with each other."[14]

IMPERFECT CHOICES

For several reasons, including mental disability, illness, depression, and insanity, some people lack the ability to make a rational decision about their sexual behavior. In 1989, four teenage boys from Glen Ridge, New Jersey, sexually exploited a young woman who had an I.Q. of only 64.[15] Even though the woman's personal makeup included a great need to please others, the boys were charged with raping her, because of her questionable ability to make decisions and to *rationally* consent to sex. Three were convicted of aggravated sexual assault

Ethics is about choice—choosing the best alternative. In some situations, people feel as though they face an impossible decision because their available choices are so terrible. For instance, a woman at gunpoint may consent to being raped in order to save her life. A wife may consent to spousal rape, hoping to spare herself and her children from a worse fate. Or, a young man or woman may run away from a terrible home life and resort to prostitution out of despair that no better choices seem to exist. These are extemely difficult moral dilemmas and they are, unfortunately, not altogether rare ones.

Let's go back to our fictional couple, Jill and Zach. Only now we'll give Jill a sexual history that includes many partners and a great deal of sexual experimentation. Zach knows about Jill's past sexual behavior. In fact, many other people know as well. What he doesn't know, however, is that while she was growing up, Jill had been molested frequently by her stepfather. At the time she met Zach, she had low self-esteem and an insatiable need for affection and attention. And Zach, mistaking her sexual permissiveness for freely given consent, failed to realize that in reality Jill was consenting to being *loved*, not to being *exploited* (even though she was, in fact, allowing him to exploit her).

Given the high incidence of incest and sexual abuse in our society, Jill is not alone. Unfortunately, many people are victims of hardship, abuse, and dysfunctional family life. Still, while these experiences may *account* for someone's behavior, do they morally *excuse* anyone for allowing himself or herself to be used for sex or for hurting or abusing others?

THE GREEN LIGHT

In response to several reported incidents of sexual violence on campus, Antioch College, a small liberal arts school in Yellow Springs, Ohio, inaugurated a sexual consent policy. In short, this clearly defined policy requires that all sexual contact and conduct between any two people must be consensual, and further, before sexual contact or conduct can occur, consent must be obtained verbally.[16] In other words, Antioch students need to ask first!

The responsibility for asking for consent lies with the person who wants to initiate a higher level of physical contact. Finally, consent must be verbally obtained each and every time the two engage in sex.

Many people believe that mutual consent is a moral green light, that anything two consenting adults do in private is all right. But the issue of consent involves much more. As the Antioch policy suggests, if one partner is under the influence of alcohol or drugs, verbal consent is meaningless. In response to this, Antioch's policy states that taking advantage of someone who is "under the influence" is never acceptable behavior.[17]

Antioch's policy was widely criticized and parodied for its lack of romance or subtlety. In addition, many people said that while the policy may work at Antioch, it does little to prepare Antioch students for the "real world." In Antioch's defense, one student pointed out that the policy was planned for Antioch in particular, a campus culture that is more liberal than that on most other campuses.[18] As another student pointed out, "The policy isn't to have 'Big Brother' looking over your shoulder," but is simply trying to create a way for partners to have a dialogue about sex.[19]

True, without consent, no sexual conduct can be moral. Yet two people *can* consent to behavior that is wrong. For instance, teachers can hold out high marks to students who consent to have sex with them. The consent is there, but for the wrong reason (assuming that it is wrong to use sex to win other favors). Similarly, asking your best friend's steady to have sex, believing that the consent puts a moral stamp of approval on the experience, is rationalization.

What about the type of sexual activity two people consent to have? Is high-risk sex, even if consensual, morally right? Is consenting to skip birth control immoral when you need to avoid pregnancy? If sadomasochistic (hurtful) sex, group sex orgies, and the like are consensual, are they also moral?

KNOWING WHEN TO BACK OFF

Let's turn to Jill and Zach one last time. We'll change the script about them, though. Instead of being at a prom weekend, Jill is twenty-three and still a virgin. She loves Zach and wants to marry him someday, though not for several more years.

Having practiced self-control for so many years, Jill is having difficulty finally agreeing to sexual intercourse. How much persuasion or coercion can Zach rightfully use to help Jill overcome her fears and inhibitions?

For those of you who believe that Zach does have a right to attempt to persuade Jill to have sex, consider these other situations: Would he have the same right to persuade her to have sex several months before their engagement? When they first fell in love? If she loves him, but he doesn't love her (or vice versa)? When they discovered they have a mutual attraction to each other? When they first met?

In all fairness to Zach, who is taking a lot of the rap, does Jill have any right to seduce *him* into having sexual intercourse? If they already are having sex, does she have any right to force him to have sex against his will if he isn't in the mood for it? Does she have the right to constantly persuade him to kiss her in public, when he is uncomfortable with that, or to engage in any sexual behavior that goes against his beliefs?

What if Zach is her tennis coach and jeopardizes his relationship with her, as well as his job, if he has a sexual relationship with her? What if Zach has broken up with her and is still attracted to her physically, but wants to stay out of a relationship with her? Indeed, is merely *asking* for sex, even when you are willing to take no for an answer, ever wrong?

One legacy of the double standard is the game people play about signals. In this situation, women feel compelled to coyly say no, when sometimes they mean maybe or yes, in order to maintain respect and not appear too loose or forward. And some men choose never to take no for an answer.

That sex requires consent in order to be moral is consistent with nearly all ethical principles. That each person alone must decide how to behave is consistent with moral freedom. But as we can see by the examples in this section (and by our laws regarding sex crimes), consent requires good communication skills. This includes learning to be fair about the questions, and honest and wise about the answers.

46

FREEDOM FOR ALL 5

During biblical days, parents arranged marriage partners for their children. Brides and grooms often met for the first time on their wedding day. Sometimes girls who were still children were betrothed to older, widowed men who had already fathered children. Or young girls were betrothed to boys just as young. For instance, Mohandas K. Gandhi, India's beloved leader, married his wife, Kasturbai, when both were only thirteen years of age.

Today, the customs of arranged marriages and young brides and grooms persist in certain regions of the world. True, many parents select wonderful mates for their children, and many children appreciate the custom, trusting their parents to choose wisely and well. Also, children may sometimes participate in the decision and reject someone who doesn't meet with their approval.

However, any custom that denies people free choice, or forces people into sexual relationships against their will, for whatever reason, including economic survival, defies a basic human principle—the right to moral autonomy (freedom) and consensual sex. Many people also believe that the traditional payment for a bride, called a dowry, is morally offensive because it implies that a woman is property.

MAKING THE RIGHT CHOICES

Even if we don't believe that other people, including our parents, have the right to choose or censor our sexual partners, how much responsibility do *we* have to choose a suitable partner by ourselves, or to take others' advice when it is reasonable? And what moral standards shall we apply to our choices?

In our society, it seems as if we expect attractive people to pair up with other attractive people.[1] (What could he possibly see in *her?*) It is even customary for people of the same stature to pair up—short men with short women, tall women with tall men. Indeed, according to the authors of *Sex in America*, most of us do choose sexual partners remarkably similar to ourselves—in age, race or ethnicity, and education.[2]

Although customary, what *moral* good is there to selecting partners on the basis of superficial criteria such as appearance, athletic ability, or wealth? Further, how right is it to let others influence our choices? (He's not "good" enough for you! What a loser! You aren't going to go out with *her*, are you?) According to the authors of the *Sex in America* study, you may benefit by choosing a partner that your peers and family approve of, since often they recognize qualities that you may have overlooked. On the other hand, family members can make life somewhat miserable for you, even shutting you out of their lives, should you go against their "rules." In fact, a couple can rarely escape the web of outsiders with opinions on whether or not their match is suitable.[3] Occasionally, the influence of peers, family, and society is so subtle that it is difficult to recognize.

The strongest taboos are against homosexual couples and interracial couples, at least among "mainstream" Americans. Thus, heterosexual people who choose partners of the same race, class, and education have a better chance of being accepted and fitting in with their peers, families, and communities, and feeling that they are sexually compatible.[4]

Still, moral autonomy (freedom to choose) requires that we make wise choices. This, at times, requires that we be independent and strong about our convictions. Likewise, moral goodness and fairness may require that we judge the choices of others with kindness, compassion, and tolerance.

In the last century, after scientists unlocked some of the secrets of heredity, a new discipline called eugenics emerged. Proponents of eugenics sought to use knowledge of the principles of heredity, and of how certain diseases and traits are passed on from generation to generation, to improve the human race and society.

To this end, eugenicists wanted to prevent "unfit" people from passing on their so-called bad qualities (negative eugenics). At the same time, they encouraged those who were considered fine physical specimens—intelligent, virtuous, and otherwise fit—to marry each other and have offspring who would resemble, and perhaps surpass, their parents' positive qualities. In this way, each succeeding generation would supposedly improve. Ultimately, genetic selection could lead to a master race of human beings who would create a perfect society.[5]

Eugenics had an influence on some politicians, and affected the way some people thought about suitable sexual partners. It also influenced Congress in passage of the Immigration Act of 1924, which restricted the number of poor Eastern Europeans who could get permission to enter the United States. (Poverty was thought to be caused by bad genes, not inadequate social, educational, or economic opportunities—a belief that persists today.)

Eugenics had an impact on Margaret Sanger's birth control agenda.[6] In her pioneering efforts to educate women about birth control, she worked specifically to help poor women from having more babies than they could handle, and eugenics inspired her to persuade these women to keep from producing any more "unfit"—that is, poor—Americans. Lastly, eugenics fostered racism, a climate of social intolerance, and legislation that prohibited interracial couples from marrying.

Few of its supporters foresaw the insidious role eugenics would play in horrors like the Holocaust and Hitler's plan to make Western Europe "racially pure." Nor did they recognize the fallacy inherent in their reasoning and policies. Besides being immoral, eugenics fails the test of reason. The kind of physical disabilities eugenicists try to "weed out" (such as cerebral palsy or epilepsy) do not make people undesirable members of society or poor parents. Raising children successfully depends largely on how well people can nurture them and teach good character, not on parents' physical health or intellectual superiority. Moreover, many people grow up in disadvantaged homes or in foster care. Yet despite the odds being stacked against them, many of these people grow up with impeccable character and fine parenting skills of their own.

Finally, eugenics fails to make a distinction between perfect people and a just society. And the distinction matters. A just society is one where people are treated well, no matter what their disabilities.

In summary, eugenics is so fallacious that it would not be worth discussing were it not for the fact that this kind of thinking has a continuing influence in our society. Whenever politicians begin to talk of welfare reform, the suggestion of compelling poor people to be sterilized, or at least to stop having children, crops up. Only recently (1994), a purportedly scholarly book, *The Bell Curve*, again dwelled on the issue of racial superiority, its thesis being that certain races are inherently more intelligent than other races, a theory that serves no purpose and stands on shaky scientific ground.

From 1907 to 1960, more than 100,000 Americans living in more than thirty states were sterilized because they were deemed unworthy to have offspring.[7] In 1994 legislators in Connecticut and Florida introduced bills to provide cash bonuses for welfare recipients who accepted Norplant (an implanted method of long-term birth control). Florida's bill also offered $400 to men living below the poverty line if they agreed to have vasectomies. And the trend toward such sterilization programs shows little sign of waning.[8]

At a school assembly in the spring of 1994, the principal of Randolph County High School in Alabama touched off a storm of protest by deciding to cancel the prom after learning that several racially mixed couples were planning to attend. Then the principal told a high school junior whose father is white and mother is black, that her parents had made a "mistake" in having her, adding that it was a mistake he hoped to prevent others from making.[9]

LIVE AND LET LIVE

Many people still believe that they have the right to stop others from choosing their own sexual partners. What right, if any, do we have to do that to other people? Or to attempt to influence them, or condemn them? Does society, for example, have the right to stop people from buying a sexual partner, as in prostitution? Even if biracial marriages are not common, does anyone have the right to stop biracial couples from marrying? What about laws against first cousins marrying, or policies that force mentally disabled teenagers to be sterilized?

Dating, marriage, and childbearing affect an entire family. A girl's date may someday be her parent's son-in-law, while her brother's steady girlfriend may someday be her sister-in-law. Does this potential for future relationships give family members any right to condemn certain choices, or express their disapproval? Do parents have any right to stop children from dating or marrying a person of a certain religious, ethnic, or socioeconomic background? Do they have the right to dissuade their children from marrying someone with a severe physical disability?

Reading a newspaper or listening to a political debate shows us that some people are offended by homosexual behavior. Some are offended by sex between people of different racial or ethnic groups. Nevertheless, does anyone have a right to actually *stop* couples from choosing each other, or to punish them for a deviation from their own moral compass? Further, we may have a right to *personally* disapprove of homosexuality and refrain from interracial dating; how does that right extend to staring and glaring at gays and mixed couples, or worse, to bashing gays or harassing interracial couples?

Another aspect of this issue of choice is masturbation (having sex with yourself). For many people, masturbation is an outlet for sexual desire, as well as a way to learn more about their own bodies. In fact, according to a University of Chicago study, the people who were most likely to have a regular sexual partner and most likely to have sex of all kinds were also most likely to masturbate. Nearly 85 percent of men and 45 percent of women who were living with a sexual partner had masturbated in the previous year.[10]

52

Many religious people regard masturbation as sinful. They have the right not to engage in it. On the other hand, do parents who disapprove of masturbation have the right to punish their children for masturbating? Do members of a religious group condemning masturbation as sinful have a right to keep educators from teaching students that mutual masturbation is a safe, healthy alternative to intercourse?

THE RIGHT TO BE CHOSEN

The right to choose has an interesting corollary—the right to be *perceived* as a sexual being. Most teenagers in our society want and need to experience physical closeness, if only to touch, hug, or kiss another person. Yet a great deal of prejudice exists against people who fail to meet our stereotypes and standards for suitable sexual partners, as though their sexuality were invisible and they were undeserving of sex.

The sexuality of obese teens, multiple amputees, and others who deviate from the able-bodied "norm" is often overlooked. Even people with superficial conditions, such as acne, stuttering, or burn scars may experience discrimination.

The easy excuse for such prejudice is that, after all, everyone deserves to feel a physical attraction to a sexual partner. However, such closed-minded thinking may deprive us of potentially valuable relationships. "Throughout my life I had remained unaware of people with disabilities," explains Erica Levy Klein, coauthor of *Enabling Romance*, a sexual manual for people with physical disabilities. "My mother had raised me to 'stay away from damaged goods' and date only perfect people with no problems—not any physical ones anyway."[11] Then Klein went out on a date with Ken Kroll, who is paralyzed and uses a wheelchair. Despite feeling attracted to his personality and the many interests they shared, Klein assumed that because Kroll was disabled, he couldn't have sex. In time, she learned that indeed he could, and they married.

Due to their reliance on physical attendants and assisted living, some people may be denied the opportunity to have sex. After Ellen Stohl survived a terrible car wreck while at college, one of her first questions was: Will I be able to have sex?[12] Stohl discovered that she could have sex and could find suitable sexual partners. In fact, she posed for a *Playboy* spread in order to dispel the myth that disabled women aren't sexy. As Christopher Voelker, who also uses a wheelchair, said when he photographed Stohl for an article in another magazine, "I showed that Ellen is a vibrant, sexually alive person. Period."[13] Despite her good looks and obvious sexuality, though, when Stohl pursued a career as an actress, few Hollywood producers gave her a chance to audition—let alone cast her, much to Stohl's frustration and outrage.

Many disabled people themselves devalue each other as sexual partners, explains Cheryl Marie Wade, a wheelchair user. "I wanted to look like an oh-so-real woman. I thought the way to do it was to have an able-bodied man love you . . . want you." Wade eventually overcame her fears, learned to accept her body and its physical limitations, and fell in love with a man who is paralyzed.[14]

FITTING THE MOLD

In societies where food is plentiful, thinner bodies set the sexual standard; while in societies with scarcities, a greater sexual value is placed on heftier body types. Although these standards are arbitrary and rel-

ative to the society, the standard of sexual attractiveness in the United States today stresses young women with firm, washboard stomachs, rounded breasts, shapely legs, and a mane of gorgeous hair. As for young men, sexy means the Greek god look—muscular definition, athleticism, and height, not to mention a healthy head of hair, too. The only problem is that few people fit these ideals.

That beauty is only skin deep may be true. But with our bodies, we project much about our sexuality. Unfortunately, impossible ideals and stereotypes create serious moral conflicts, for example: what measures should a person take to feel and be sexually attractive, both in general and to someone in particular?

Now, exercise, good nutrition, and grooming may improve a person's health and body image. Repairing crossed eyes or correcting a clubfoot improves a person's well-being and enhances self-esteem at the same time. Hormone therapy, and cosmetic and other surgery, can even give people the choice of changing their sexuality and gender altogether.

Often, however, at grave risk to their health, fertility, or their lives, people resort to drastic measures. Many binge on and purge food to attain or maintain unnatural thinness. Others exercise excessively, or have their breasts enlarged with implants of uncertain long-term safety.

To improve their athletic builds, as well as their sex appeal, some bodybuilders take anabolic steroids. And to acquire an air of sophistication, or to maintain their low weight, many people resort to a smoking habit. Other practices gaining popularity among young people are tattooing and body piercing, particularly in sensitive or sexual areas of the body, such as lips, tongues, navels, nipples, and genitals.

Granted, some of these attempts to alter the body are harmless and may improve a person's sex appeal; others carry risks. Unfortunately, the use of anabolic steroids or a smoking habit can seriously impair a person's future health.

Many people experience an instant attraction to each other, a physical "chemistry," based on appearance. Others are turned off by a single physical characteristic before giving a person who may have many fine qualities a chance. They say: "I like only girls with small butts" or "I hate guys with short, stubby feet," as though physical details have anything to do with the real person.

No one has the right to dictate to whom you should or should not be physically attracted. Nor is it fair to make judgments about people from their appearance, or, worse, to make anyone feel so terrible about themselves that they are willing to risk their health or life to meet your superficial standards.

Some girls with large breasts and comely figures enjoy the sexual attention their bodies elicit. But others complain that by focusing on their body, particularly their large breasts, boys fail to respect the person who has the body. In turn, men focus too much attention and worry on penis size, despite the fact that size has little to do with sexual gratification.

CONFORMING TO CULTURE

At the extreme end of the issue of sexual choice is a widespread but, until recent years, seldom discussed foreign custom prevalant in more than 25 nations.[15] This is the custom of female genital circumcision, in which the clitoris and labia are cut away and, in many cases, the vagina is stitched closed to the size of a pinhole. Female circumcision is frequently performed with crude instruments in unsanitary conditions. The girls are held down by women, as the exceedingly painful procedure is performed without anesthesia.

Why? Why would a parent expose a daughter to such mutilation? Primarily, the procedure is done to ensure men that their brides will be virgins and, also, as one father said, to guarantee that this woman "will later on . . . behave herself."[16] Or, as an immigrant mother from Mali on trial in France for having her three-month-old baby circumcised explained, she did it for her child's future welfare, "to make her like the other girls so that she could find a husband." The infant nearly died from complications.[17]

Unlike male circumcision, which is a relatively harmless procedure (although some people argue against this ritual), female circumcision—particularly the more radical form in which nearly all external genitilia are removed—has tragic consequences for nearly every one of its victims.

Most women who undergo circumcision never feel sexual desire, achieve orgasm, or experience the joy of sex. The procedure is excruciatingly painful and carries a serious risk of infection. Female cir-

57

cumcision frequently causes lifelong complications, including hard scars, cysts, and swellings, and difficulty bearing children, urinating, or menstruating. And some females die from it.

The social consequences for *un*circumcised women in societies where the custom prevails are so severe that, caught between a rock and a hard place, most mothers and grandmothers voluntarily carry on the tradition. Without circumcision, girls have little opportunity to marry, leaving them few options in their largely patriarchal communities besides prostitution or destitution.

Sexual practices are regarded as personal choice and foreign customs considered none of our business. But because so many females are affected—80 million worldwide, many of them children—and because the practice is tantamount to "sexual torture, maiming, deprivation, and life-shortening illness," *New York Times* columnist A. M. Rosenthal implores us to speak out and take a stand against it.

"I do not understand why more Americans, particularly women and African Americans, do not raise absolute hell about it with the U.N. and African governments," laments Rosenthal.[18] Or, as Linda Weil-Curiel, a French prosecutor who has been waging a crusade against the custom in France and England, says, "If immigrants cut off a girl's ear in the name of tradition, there would be an outcry. But here the sex of a future woman is cut off and people are willing to defend it or turn away." Adds Weil-Curiel, "It is up to women to force the issue onto government agendas."[19]

Athough disapproving observers may define sexual freedom as having many partners or promiscuous sex, the term basically means the freedom to choose sexual partners or to choose to abstain from sex and from marriage. And like the freedoms guaranteed by our constitution and the United Nations Bill of Human Rights, sexual freedom should include equality, justice, and freedom *for all.*

HIGH ON THE MOUNTAIN OF LOVE

Since school began, Rachel and Brian had been an item. Now Rachel is cooling off, but she has yet to tell Brian or break up with him. Over Thanksgiving, Rachel meets Brian's brother Scott, who is home on leave from the Navy.

As the weekend wears on, Rachel feels a growing attraction for Scott. Maybe it was the way he looked directly at her when he talked. Maybe it was the way he smelled of hickory from chopping wood for the fireplace. Or maybe it was the way he told those outrageous stories of life in the barracks, reminding her of stories her grandfather used to tell.

Whatever the spell, by the time Brian drove Rachel home, her mind was racing with thoughts of Scott, of their conversations, his laughter, even the memory of his scent. She found herself imagining what it would be like to kiss him or welcome him back after a long absence.

That night, Rachel tossed and turned, unable to sleep or to stop

dwelling on thoughts of Scott. I'm not married to Brian, she told herself. We've only been dating two and a half months. What could be so bad about breaking up with him and dating his brother?

With over five billion people on this planet, it is easy to tell Rachel to fall for someone else besides her current boyfriend's brother. Once people become infatuated with another person, however, all they want is that one person—their beloved. And, just like the salmon who swim against tremendous barriers to reach their spawning grounds, no obstacle will seem too high to overcome, no fault too terrible to accept, no taboo strong enough to keep them apart.

Beginning in their teen years, Americans are expected and encouraged to form close relationships with other teenagers. Even those who do not pair off find many social opportunities. At parties, dances, and just hanging out with other people, they look for sex and love.

One of the primary purposes of dating, as Stanley Grentz suggests in his book *Sexual Ethics*, is to build a healthy relationship that can foster each person's growth.[1] Dating also gives a teenager experience in choosing a suitable lifetime companion. These underlying reasons make the experience valuable.

As we might expect, the attraction between Rachel and Scott intensified over the long weekend. By the time Thanksgiving vacation ended, Rachel had broken up with Brian—who was stunned, angry, and feeling deeply betrayed by the loss of his girlfriend to his brother. In fact, relations deteriorated to the point where no one except Rachel and Scott were speaking. While they felt constrained by the tension they had caused, the situation actually intensified the passion Rachel and Scott felt for each other, as if their love was fated to survive any obstacle.

Perhaps if Rachel or Scott had recognized the early signs of what is a nearly universal phenomenon—the courtship ritual—and understood how deeply their betrayal would wound Brian, they might have flirted less and exercised more self-control over their behavior. That way, they could have channeled their feelings for each other into a platonic (no sex) friendship instead of a romance. Or could they?

Morality requires taking control of our behavior, even during those times when we feel as though our emotions or sex drives are on a course of their own. And indeed, according to the many scientists who study sexual behavior and courtship, we have an incredibly strong biological destiny for flirtation, infatuation, and love. Without these, in fact, our species would hardly survive.[2]

From their studies of courtship and mating, anthropologists (scientists who study the origin and the physical, social, and cultural development and behavior of human beings) have discovered that certain mating gestures, such as the coy look, head toss, chest thrust, and intense gaze, are universal to all human beings, and are even seen in nonhuman species.[3]

In two different studies of American singles, David Givens and Timothy Perper each observed a distinct pattern of courtship.[4] Apparently, as people in search of a partner meet for the first time, they behave in a rather predictable pattern as they develop a sexual and emotional attachment to each other.

ON THE PLAYING FIELD

In the first stage of this courtship pattern, people use body language to signal their availability for sex or romance. Men may pat their hair, adapt a swaggering walk, or exaggerate their body movements. Women get attention by a particular stance, or by coyly tilting their heads or puckering their lips.

In the next stage, people try to make eye contact by looking into the other person's eyes a few seconds longer than is customary, perhaps smiling, too. (This contact can be so powerful that married Orthodox Jewish men are prohibited from looking directly into the eyes of any women other than their wives.) When two people feel comfortable looking at each other so unabashedly, they move on to the next and probably most critical stage—talking.

Here one party will strike up a conversation, often with a trite starter like "Haven't we met before?" or "You look like someone I know," and other questions, compliments, or comments. People's words and voices offer strong clues about themselves, from their social background and education to particular personality and character traits. This "grooming talk," as British anthropologist Desmond Morris has dubbed this stage, will either attract or repel the listener, and can therefore either end a potential relationship or inspire someone to continue.

Once they have passed this initial stage, our couple will engage in more meaningful conversation—for hours and often to the exclusion of anyone around them. As they hold onto each other's words, perhaps laughing more than usual and flirting, they move into the final stage—touching.

Starting with innocent behavior, such as leaning forward as they listen or touching the other person lightly on the arm when making a point, our couple unconsciously uses simple body language to connect to each other on an emotional level.

If the attraction continues to escalate, a fascinating phenomenon—synchrony—occurs, where a couple's movements begin to mirror each other. If one leans to the side or crosses a leg, for example, the other person may do the same thing. Synchrony is integral to courtship and mating. Dance and music allow people to synchronize to the same rhythm; this may explain why they are part of nearly every culture that allows its members some choice over their sexual partners.

The process of courtship can end abruptly, any time one party loses interest or deliberately stops participating. Also, many people pass through these stages rather cautiously and slowly. In fact, someone who tries to move in too fast or act too aggressively can cause the other person to turn away.

Why study such mating games or care how they function? There is an important reason: during the earliest stages, if people can see and understand exactly what is taking place, they can make a conscious decision to leave the "playing field." Why, though? If dating and mating are so important, why inhibit what may turn into an intense love affair?

There are many reasons to screech to a halt. If the person "coming on" is your teacher, coach, therapist, employer, religious leader, or the like, the relationship can cause serious harm or disruption, and in cases where minors are involved, be a crime. If the relationship involves a person with a reputation for using or abusing people, putting on the brakes early can spare you pain and grief.

If people like Rachel or Scott realize how much control they could exercise, then they would not see themselves as "helplessly in love." Such knowledge might spare them and Brian the pain, guilt, jealousy, betrayal, and mistrust their triangle will cause. Indeed, at the earliest stages (but perhaps *only* then), people can exit from a potential relationship without devastating another person or suffering needlessly over the loss.

Once two people develop a strong desire to pursue each other, it is usually too late to extinguish the flame of desire without pain. After a strong attraction develops, in fact, a couple probably will have a nearly insatiable desire to hold hands, walk arm-in-arm, hug, and kiss. In time, sexual desire intensifies, and a couple may find themselves head-over-heels in love.

As the relationship grows, couples desire more physical and sexual intimacy. Rarely can a couple intensely in love stop doing what they have already done, or retreat to an earlier stage. Yet for teenagers in love who want to retain their sexual innocence—especially as passion courses through their veins—the need to exercise *tremendous* restraint is great, because *it is so very natural to act otherwise.*

TRUE LOVE

Infatuation begins the moment another person takes on a special meaning.[5] After that, as Rachel experienced with Scott, images of that person, songs you both like, fantasies of a future together, increasingly occupy your mind. For many people, such "intrusive thinking" about their loved one consumes more and more of their time, and in a few cases, nearly all their waking hours.

Why *did* Rachel flip for Scott? Was it the way he flirted with her? Was it because he laughed at her witticisms or loved to fly kites on windy days, as she loved to do? Or was it because his storytelling reminded her of the grandfather she adored?

According to John Money, a prominent sexologist (someone who studies sexual behavior), we fall in love with people who match what he calls our "love map"—the specific portrait of an ideal love that we develop from our childhood experiences.[6] The details of this ideal person can be shaped by the scent, personality, and appearance of our parents, the turmoil or tranquility of our home life,  unique characteristics of our relatives and friends, happy moments we experienced in childhood, and our favorite places. Together, they create a picture, shaped, also, by negative experiences (which partially explains the reason some people always seem to choose partners who are wrong for them).

In the same way that we develop a cultural preference for certain foods such as pizza, and an abhorrence for other foods, we also develop preferences for a person of a particular culture or ethnic group. Hence, people who grow up among an ethnic group that values humor or intellect will seek these traits in a person. Further, we tend to be drawn to people like ourselves, who share our particular values, interests, and many of our traits.

Success in love depends on finding someone who fits our image of an ideal lover, and whose image we, in turn, fit. However, falling in love requires more than a simple match, as Helen Fisher explains in her book *Anatomy of Love*.[7] According to Fisher, timing is essential: We need to be *ready* for love. Those people who are eager for adventure, romance, or a meaningful relationship, and those who feel lonesome or hurt from a previous failed relationship are more likely to fall in love than are people who neither want nor need a new relationship.

Another factor is novelty or mystery. While many people meet friends through people they already know, they are more inclined to fall in love with someone who is relatively new to them than with someone they have known all their lives. Thus, although close friendships occasionally blossom into love, the chances of a longtime friendship's doing so are slim. Consequently, people looking for love need to look outside their close circle of friends to meet new people. However, the odds of falling in love and having a long-term relationship tend to improve when those new people have achieved the same education level, and are of the same social class and race, and even a similar age.[8]

Ironically, there is nothing like a hurdle to intensify our emotional attachment to another person. Obstacles in the love field include parental disapproval, forced separations, and other deterrents. At the same time, obstacles such as strong family disapproval, where families threaten to disown a person for their choice of partner, can, in the long run, contribute to the couple's split.

If love maps converge and the timing is right, if two people find each other against what appear to be great odds, if a scent, or a dance, strike a pleasant enough cord, then, pow . . . we have instant love. Whether it is love at first sight or the slow, steady evolution of emotions, loving someone and being loved by that person is one of the most ecstatic of all human experiences.

HIGH ON THE MOUNTAIN OF LOVE

Madly in love. Infatuated. Lovesick.

Falling in love appears to be part of our genetic program, a way of ensuring that most of us will mate and produce offspring. Psychiatrist Michael Liebowitz suspects that our brains actully produce a chemistry of love.[9]

According to Liebowitz, the state of exaltation we experience is partly due to a chemical saturation of PEA (phenylthalamine) on the neurons of the cortex, the part of the brain controlling our emotions. PEA is a naturally produced amphetamine that speeds up the brain's connections and causes the excited state of mind that a person feels when he or she first falls in love. This is what gives lovers the ability to stay awake all night and caress; to be amorous, intense, euphoric, and occasionally out of control. It can also cause intense doubt. In short, the brain chemistry of a person in love creates the roller coaster of emotions that lovers typically feel.

Infatuation rarely lasts long.[10] When it slows down, it can be replaced by a different state of being—attachment. Here, other brain chemicals called endorphins (which are opiates) saturate the neuron endings. Rather than stimulate us as the amphetamines did, endorphins calm us down and give us peace of mind. "Now lovers can talk and eat and sleep in peace," observes Liebowitz.[11]

As they might do with other chemical reactions, some people become addicted to infatuation. As a result, they may fail to value the quieter, longer-lasting kind of love. Preferring the thrill of infatuation, they constantly fall in and out of love. Then, as their emotions calm down, they leave the relationship, a departure that frequently leaves a partner stunned and hurt.

Teenagers often find themselves unable to make permanent commitments to a relationship so early in their lives. Furthermore, as their relationships lose their luster, they need to be able to leave them. For some teens, love may not come as soon as they think it should. But the recipe for infatuation is complex, after all. And life offers many years in which to find someone to love, who can return that love. In the meantime, there are many ways to prepare for love, mainly by forming deep friendships and learning to care about other people.

PART OF THE DEAL

A person who is loved may, for any number of reasons, choose not to return the affection. Just as people have the right to consent to sex, they also have a right to choose when and whom to love. Moreover, all single persons (and there are those who would argue married persons, as well) have a right to end a relationship when love ends. This is probably one of the most difficult principles to accept. Many scorned lovers have a hard time hearing and accepting the message.

Furthermore, while everyone has the right to pursue a true love, that right hardly extends to making a nuisance of oneself (no matter what movies or novels show us). Clearly, it is never right to demand, threaten, extort, or harass another person to return your love.

Despite the popular adage "love is blind," most lovers are aware of their partner's shortcomings.[12] Yet, in a process called crystallization, they selectively ignore or dismiss their lover's faults. Because of this, many people stay in abusive or neglectful relationships. Or they stay out of fear of what their lover will do if they leave. Indeed, jealous or angry lovers may threaten to seriously harm or even kill a partner who scorns or tries to leave them, as is alleged in cases like that of O. J. Simpson and his ex-wife, Nicole Brown.

Anyone who loves you has the duty to treat you kindly, respectfully, and safely. You, in turn, have the same responsibility. If either they or you fail on this measure, you owe it to yourself to find the strength, resolve, and support to leave the relationship or mend your ways.

WHAT'S LOVE GOT TO DO WITH IT?

A chaste love affair is one where sex is absent. While frustrating, such relationships can be intensely passionate. Indeed, not being able to have sexual relations, even to touch or kiss, can fuel passion to incredible heights. Some of our most romantic stories, myths, and poems rhapsodize such sexually unfulfilled love affairs.

In contrast, many people have sex *without* love or affection. Or, people have sex *in order* to get love, hoping that by having sex, their partner will care more about them. To paraphrase sex educator Mary Calderone's wry observation: Girls use sex to get love and boys use love to get sex.[13] And while more women than men believe that love is essential in a sexual relationship, most men and women find it difficult to have sex without any emotional involvement at all.[14]

Being needy for love and affection drives many people into sexual partnerships with people who are unworthy of their attention, affection, or intimacy. People who routinely engage in such encounters risk losing their self-esteem and their ability to make a long-term commitment should a suitable partner come into their lives. It also

69

causes people to use others in order to release sexual tension, with little regard or consideration for their partner's well-being. Ultimately, sex for love and love for sex lay a foundation of dishonesty in a relationship.

What if Rachel and Brian had broken up—not because of Scott, but simply because their romance had faded away? Does a past sexual history give them the right to engage in sex now, if one or both of them feel like it?

What if Rachel and Brian had never had a sexual relationship, but had just been platonic (nonsexual) friends instead? Would having sex together ruin their friendship? Or, what if Rachel and Brian got drunk and then had sex? Would that mistake give either one the right, after being such good friends, to end the friendship?

If Rachel and Brian are just friends, does Brian have the right to flirt with Rachel and entice her to fall in love with him? Knowing that she has no sexual interest in him, does he have any right to flirt with her or make sexual innuendos?

Let's say Rachel falls in love with Brian. If he is gay, does he have any responsiblity to inform her that his sexual orientation excludes her—not because of her in particular, but because she is not male?

Some people believe that there is nothing wrong with anonymous sex, that it is okay to kiss or neck with acquaintances or even total strangers at a party. And a few couples who start out with such emotional indifference do eventually fall in love with each other. Does this possibility justify sex without affection? Or does sex without affection require justification?

If we believe the anthropologists who say that we have a biological destiny for sex and love, although many religious people refuse to subscribe to such Darwinian theories, we can let nature take its course. We can allow our hormones, brain chemicals, and emotional needs to control our sexual behavior. Some claim that they will anyway, no matter how much effort we make to overcome them.

Just as we can temper our sexual conduct, though, we can temper our choice of sexual partners. Of course, given the nature of love, such temperance can be exceedingly difficult.

Contrary to what some people say, no one has a moral obligation to change his or her sexual orientation. Regardless of whether they are heterosexual, homosexual, or bisexual, all persons have the right to pick suitable partners, as well as a responsibility to themselves to leave an abusive relationship, no matter how much they love their partner or feel the need for a relationship. They owe it to themselves to learn how to avoid such relationships in the future and to leave any that do occur.

It can take all the courage you can muster and all the help you can find to break off a love relationship or recover from the hurt of being jilted. To do this, some people, especially those with a long history of abuse, neglect, and failed relationships, may require professional, religious, or spiritual guidance.

Finding an outlet for sexual tension instead of finding an unsuitable partner is also a challenge—especially when the desire to be with someone, anyone, overtakes our patience to wait for a suitable partner.

Love may be blind, but morality requires clear navigation, the ability to avoid mistakes before they get out of hand, and the fortitude to end a bad relationship when it does occur. The challenge is also to find suitable partners, worthy of our love and sexual intimacy, and to refrain from hurting or using those people who mistakenly cross our pathway to true love.

AIN'T NOBODY'S BUSINESS IF I DO

Sex is a personal issue that we tend to regard as a strictly private affair. When sexual behavior does not affect other people, we have the right to question laws and policies that suggest that it does. However, when sexual behavior affects others, it is no longer a private issue.

For example, the actual risk of acquiring H.I.V. from a single unprotected (vaginal) sexual contact with an infected person may be 1 in 500.[1] Yet, Alison Gertz, of New York City, failed to beat those odds. As a result of a single encounter she had when she was sixteen years old, Ms. Gertz acquired AIDS. During the course of her illness and after her death, Gertz's family and friends faced untold grief. Her brief sexual encounter was hardly a private affair.

Despite the consequences, millions of Americans play the same game of Russian roulette, with the innocent assumption that nobody else has a moral claim on their private sexual behavior.

However, today AIDS is the sixth leading cause of death among young persons aged 15 to 24.[2] Other sexually transmitted diseases, while not as life-threatening as AIDS, have also reached epidemic proportions.

Each year, one out of four sexually active teens acquires a sexually transmitted disease such as genital herpes, which is caused by the herpes simplex virus.[3] Because there is no cure for genital herpes, all future partners of an infected person will have to protect themselves *forever* in their relationship. Some men and women who are infected with an STD will later suffer from infertility, and this condition will seriously affect their future partners, especially those who yearn to have children.

As a result of sexually transmitted diseases, many teens will suffer—if not sooner, then later—serious health problems, including infertility (inability to become pregnant or to produce sperm), ectopic pregnancies (pregnancy outside the uterus), cancer, and chronic (long-term) pain. Some, like Gertz and her partner, will die. And as it was for Gertz's family, the aftermath of their sexual encounters will have far-reaching effects.

The medical complications and emotional pain are not the only burdens to bear. Over $4 billion, much of that expense born by taxpayers and outsiders who had nothing to do with the sexual experience, will be spent each year in treatment for sexually transmitted diseases and the complications they cause.[4]

More teens than ever before are taking precautions, and this is especially true for their first sexual encounters. Nevertheless, 800,000 teenagers a year have sexual intercourse without using birth control.[5] And 1 million teens a year find themselves pregnant, primarily because they used contraception methods improperly, used unreliable contraception, or failed to use any at all.[6]

Consider that every year:

- one-tenth of all sexually active girls age 14 or younger get pregnant
- one-fifth of all sexually active girls age 15 to 17 get pregnant
- by the time they celebrate their nineteenth birthday, one in four girls will have been pregnant. Two years later, twice that many will have been pregnant.[7]

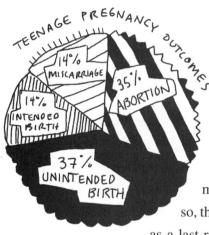

What happens to these pregnancies? Approximately 15 percent of the girls will miscarry, and a third—primarily those who can afford it—will choose to end the pregnancy by abortion.[8]

Abortion is a legal right. Although many people feel that abortion is wrong, many others believe it is a moral choice. Even so, they believe that abortion should be used only as a last resort and not as a method of birth control. Furthermore, no matter how "right" the decision to abort feels, many women and their partners suffer emotional pain and guilt in the aftermath, sometimes even years or decades later.

As for those who give birth, fewer than 3 percent place their babies up for adoption,[9] which can be positive for the adopting parents but may be heartwrenching for the biological mother and father, and grandparents.

Even among adults, the majority of babies (55 percent) come as a "surprise" to their parents.[10] All right, many of these worrisome surprises bring forth children who more than compensate for any sacrifice their parents and others will make on their behalf. And some teenagers intentionally get pregnant because they want to have a baby. Yet given the level of their education and their lack of job skills as well as maturity, teenage parents face particularly difficult obstacles in parenting, no matter how welcome their babies are.

If they marry—and only one in ten of these teenage mothers do—their marriage has an overwhelming chance of failure.[11] Married or not, deciding to finish high school or seek a higher education requires considerable resources and support from families, schools, and communities. For most teens, financially supporting a child is difficult, and requires outside help. Many teen parents are compelled to either live at home with their families or depend on public assistance.[12]

More teen boys than girls claim to be sexually active.[13] And many teenage girls, especially the young ones, get pregnant against their will or by partners who are already out of their teens.[14] Still, pregnancy—and fatherhood—affects many adolescent boys.

When Tina told Paul that she was pregnant, his first reaction was denial.[15] "It must be a joke," he thought. Even though he had had sexual relations with Tina, it was only a few times. He hardly knew her well enough to share parenting with her!

As the truth set in, Paul panicked. After all, his affair with Tina was short-lived, and being a father is a forever deal. Teen fathers are required to pay child support for eighteen years (which is longer than Paul had lived). But the *moral* responsibility of parenting has no limits. Just as it is for the families of teenage mothers, the families of teenage fathers are likely to be affected. So, too, are any future spouses of those teenage parents.

Many young fathers must be dragged into court to prove the paternity of a child. Afterward, they often have to be constantly pressured into contributing child support, a burden that is shared by the judicial system, taxpayers, and families of teen mothers.

The majority (80 percent) of children born to single teenage mothers—whether the babies were planned or unplanned—spend their childhoods living in poverty or in low economic conditions.[16]

Still, money is not the only issue. As a result of the risks their parents took, many babies are born with gonorrhea, syphilis, herpes, HIV, or are addicted to crack or heroin. Thousands of others will suffer physical and mental impairments. To raise a baby born with such serious health problems requires enormous energy, resources, and considerable outside assistance.

It is easy to believe that we are private citizens, that no one else, from family members to the government, has the right to make moral claims on us. However, we must recognize that *so* many other people will share the costs and responsibility of raising the children, especially those born with disabilities and diseases caused by sexual risk-taking. Others will be called upon to take care of the children while the parents work, finish school, or need a break; to contribute to the cost of food, housing, and health care, as well as other needs if young parents cannot or do not provide for them. With these realities, sexual intercourse is clearly not a totally private affair.

Thus, what responsibility for protecting themselves, or even restraining themselves from sexual intercourse, do teens have to their families and communities who will share the consequences of their sexual conduct? Moreover, since they will be sharing in the responsibilities, what duty do those families and groups have in return, to help teenagers avoid the pitfalls of sexual encounters?

Do parents and schools, for example, have any responsibility to offer sexual education to teenagers? If so, what kind of education should that be? One that teaches only abstinence, or one that teaches how to minimize the risks of sexual behavior and find alternatives to intercourse?

Do parents, schools, or communities have the responsibility to make free condoms available, or offer testing for sexually transmitted diseases, and exams to fit diaphragms, implant Norplant, and offer other services?

Should schools provide day care and parenting classes to those student parents who need to complete their education?

PLAYING IT SAFE

More teens than ever are using condoms, spermicides, and other forms of sexual precautions. Nonetheless, many teens take no such measures, fail to use them consistently or properly, or depend on highly unreliable methods, such as withdrawal.[17] And from what we know of the epidemic number of cases each year of sexually transmitted diseases (3 million teens will acquire a sexually transmitted disease each year[18]), both men and women knowingly and unknowingly fail to protect themselves or warn their partners of their own health status. Thus the risk of unprotected sex is substantial.

A single act of unprotected intercourse with an infected partner carries the following odds: 500:1 for acquiring H.I.V.; 30:1 for getting genital herpes; and 2:1 for contracting gonorrhea.[19] Within a year, a sexually active teen who never uses birth control has a 90 percent chance of becoming pregnant.[20]

Used properly, condoms alone can prevent 98 percent—nearly all—of unplanned pregnancies and a significant number of cases of sexually transmitted disease.[21] Even the *imperfect* use of condoms can cut risks in half.[22] (On the other hand, condoms do not offer complete protection against genital herpes, genital warts, or crabs.) If protection such as condoms is so effective and so easy to obtain, why don't more teens use it?

While it is not true that teens see themselves as immune to risk, several studies show they do have an interesting perspective on risk taking—similar, in fact, to that of most adults. Both teens and adults tend to underestimate their vulnerability to getting mugged, becoming alcoholics, having car accidents, and the like.[23] "Despite parents' qualms, teens are about as good—or bad—at appraising risk as their parents," observes Dr. Baruch Fischoff, a psychologist at Carnegie Mellon University in Pittsburgh. "It's not that teens are great at it [judging risks] but they're not any worse than we grown-ups. We all feel invulnerable to some degree."[24]

Several critical factors contribute to poor decision making and the superstitious gamble that "it can't or won't happen to me." As Dr. Fischoff explains, "A teenager may understand the dangers of driving while drunk but mistakenly thinks that beer isn't as intoxicating as other kinds of liquor."[25] Similarly, teenagers put too much trust in partners to tell them the truth, ignoring the possibility that the person they love may lie to them. Many teens also erroneously believe that they can spot a sexual disease, or know if they have contracted one. Yet STD infections can go undetected for months or years.

Sexual morality requires an ability to make wise decisions and weigh the benefits of sex against its dangers. It also requires facing up to the fact that there is no such thing as safe nonmarital sex; there is only safer sex. Most of all, morality requires *learning to control your behavior and avoid rationalizing away your moral responsibility to others, or ignoring their moral claims on your sexual conduct.*

Many people advocate abstinence as the only responsible protection against the risks of sex. Their argument has logic: If you don't have sexual intercourse, you won't get pregnant and you lessen the chances of contracting a sexually transmitted disease.

True enough. But recognizing the strong desire of many teens to experience sex, and the availability of relatively effective safeguards such as condoms, is abstinence a realistic goal? Sociologist Ira Reiss suggests otherwise. "Vows of abstinence," observes Reiss, "break far more easily than do condoms."[26]

Given the fact that the responsibility for pregnancy and STD does fall on many shoulders, shouldn't prevention also be a shared responsibility? Many parents prefer to bear the total responsibility for sex education. Too often, though, these parents neglect the lessons; or some teach only abstinence, withholding information on alternatives to sexual intercourse and how to avoid pregnancy and disease. In fact, many parents make it difficult for their teens to even mention sex.

Other parents expect the schools to share the responsibility for sex education. But only about half the states in the United States include sex education in their required curriculum, and fewer offer access to birth control or protection against STD.[27]

According to several studies, sex education combined with access to health clinics that help young people obtain protection against pregnancy and disease offer the best approach. In a model program in Baltimore, Maryland, teens who had a sex education course and access to health clinics were compared to teenagers who had no program of the sort. Within the model program, the pregnancy rate dropped by 50 percent and many of the teens postponed having sexual intercourse.[28]

Despite the success of these programs in reducing teenage pregnancy rates, New York City's plan to distribute free condoms met strong opposition. As a result, the schools could offer only a diluted effort—parents who did not want their teenagers to receive free condoms had the right to exclude their children from the program.

What about abortion? Do health insurance providers or governments have any responsibility to help pay the costs of an abortion? After all, one of the reasons that so many poor and low-income teenage girls give birth is that an abortion, which may cost five hundred dollars or more, is beyond their means. While many religious people believe that abortion is wrong, it remains a legal right, although one that, for all practical purposes, is out of the reach of poor teenagers.

Finally, what responsibility does the government have to teenagers? In 1994, Donna Shalala, secretary of health and human services, affirmed the federal government's commitment to deal with problems of teenage pregnancies and sexually transmitted diseases. "If we had a cholera epidemic," stated Shalala, "I would be out there telling people to boil water. If we had a plague, I would be helping to get rid of rats. It is important for us to step out beyond the bury-your-head strategy of the last twelve years. . . . We *do* know how to prevent H.I.V. infection. To keep this information hidden under a rug is immoral!"[29]

Others, primarily from the conservative sectors in our society, disagree, claiming that government has no moral authority to be involved in our personal sexual lives; that doing so undermines a parents' rights to impart their personal morals to their adolescent children.

While the responsibility ought to be shared, until or unless it is, it behooves all teens, for both practical and moral reasons, to accept the responsibilities themselves. And there isn't any way around that.

BIG BROTHER IN THE BEDROOM

In addition to laws against forced sex, it has always been public policy in our country to pass laws against other sexual behavior that is regarded as immoral and indecent. Adultery, homosexual relations, oral and anal sex, and fornication, for example, are illegal in many states.

Prostitution is generally illegal. A few states have recently enacted laws against marital rape and against knowingly transmitting venereal disease to an uninformed sexual partner. In all states, masturbation is legal in private, but mutual masturbation is a crime in some states, while in nearly all states masturbation in public is regarded as indecent exposure.[30]

Certainly, sexual behavior that seriously harms others, such as rape, incest, and sexual harassment, belongs within the sphere of the law. Might other behavior, though—particularly private sexual behavior between two consenting adults—fall outside the public scope and beyond its boundaries? Indeed, how much right does "Big Brother" have in our bedrooms?

At one time, sodomy was considered so "detestable and abominable [a] vice . . . committed by mankind or beast"[31] that it was a felony punishable by death, no exceptions allowed. Even when our Bill of Rights was written and adopted, the death penalty for sodomy remained. Penal reform and the humanitarian effort to abolish cruel and unusual punishment ultimately eroded such harsh legislation, until it was limited to a few years in prison and a fine.

Because sodomy was considered such a degrading crime, its legal description was coached in vague language, such as "crime against nature" or "buggery." Moreover, it covered a number of meanings, ranging from homosexual acts and oral and anal sex to bestiality (sex with animals) and necrophilia (sex with corpses). In 1961, all fifty states still outlawed sodomy, and the Sexual Offenses Act of 1967 ensured that all homosexual acts, and sodomy, gross indecency, and procurement remained criminal.

SODOMY, THE CRIME

Modern times. Modern decisions. Historical roots. Michael Hardwick is making love to a man in the bedroom of his home. A police officer enters the home and, through a partially open bedroom door, sees Hardwick having sex with another man. The officer arrests Hardwick and his partner on charges of sodomy.

Hardwick now faces a maximum prison sentence of twenty years. With the prospect of this harsh sentence, Hardwick decides to challenge the constitutionality of his state's statute against sodomy. After losing his case in a federal district court, he appeals to a higher court. Eventually, his case reached the Supreme Court, as *Bowers* v. *Hardwick*, 478 US 186, 194 (1986).

In a close (5 to 4) vote, Hardwick loses. Both Justice Byron R.

White, who wrote the majority opinion, and Justice Lewis Powell, who cast the pivotal vote, reason that conduct which has been condemned for hundreds of years, as sodomy has been, cannot now become a fundamental right. And so, sodomy remains a crime, regardless of how many millions of Americans practice it and believe that it is right.

The homosexual community is not the only victim of the law against sodomy. During his trial for purportedly raping his estranged wife, Jim Mosely admitted to engaging in oral sex with her on previous occasions. He was acquitted of the rape charges, but because oral sex is a crime in Georgia, Mosely was convicted and sentenced to five years' imprisonment. He spent two years in jail before becoming eligible for parole.

Legality, as we know from our civil rights lessons, does not automatically engender approval for behavior. Neither, as we have learned from the front line of the abortion controversy, can the judicial system resolve certain moral debates. Yet, if laws do not reflect our society's ethical standards, what *will* ensure that we achieve a moral society—or at least aspire to be one?

When any game of sexual roulette risks pregnancy, childbirth, illness, and the like, our right to privacy competes with the moral claims of all those who will share responsibility for such consequences—both the people who know us well and the public at large.

On the other hand, when we are in the position of accepting total responsibility for our behavior—when our sexual conduct is mutual and hurts no one—why should anyone else have a moral claim on our private life? Still, while mutual consent may be relatively easy to obtain, it is not easy to be sure a sexual act will affect *absolutely no one else*.

8

LIKE A VIRGIN

Many moral rules derive from a society's customs. As the customs change, confusion may arise over what is right and wrong. For example, valuing virginity has long been a custom. Is it one that is outdated, or is it still relevant? Is virginity a moral good? Some people, in jest, might even ask whether virginity is merely a lack of opportunity. Others will fail to see the humor in this statement.

In contrast, in societies where women are sheltered from public life, where their faces are hidden behind veils, away from public view, virginity is a serious concern. There, the lack of virginity in an unmarried young woman may dramatically affect her entire life, since nonvirgins may be deemed unacceptable as prospective wives.

To understand the issue of virginity, and whether it is a custom, a virtue, or merely a state of sexual innocence, it may help to look at how it was viewed in the past.

When women were regarded as property, their virginity was

highy valued. Anyone caught "stealing" the virginity of a young girl could be legally compelled to marry her and pay her father restitution. Her father could accept payment but retained the option of refusing to let his daughter marry her seducer.[1]

Long ago, a woman not only had to maintain her virginity until she found a husband but, on her wedding night, she also needed to show proof that she was indeed a virgin. Brides who failed to stain the sheet (which, incidentally, does not prove or disprove virginity) faced dire consequences. Her husband could have the marriage annulled (ended) and could return the bride to her father. He might also be eligible to receive compensation for his so-called damaged goods, while his rejected bride could be subjected to harsh punishment such as stoning.[2]

In Colonial times, the situation was somewhat more relaxed, perhaps due to the hardship of life in the New World. In some colonies, sex between courting or engaged couples was widespread and was actually tolerated. According to medical historian John Duffy, at least a third of all firstborn children were delivered within six or seven months of their parents' marriage.[3] Nonetheless, except in Rhode Island and Plymouth colonies, a male who was guilty of fornicating before marriage could be fined and the woman publicly humiliated and put into the stocks.[4]

Eventually, at least in the United States, lack of virginity at marriage was no longer a crime, although virginity remained a valued status. The grandmothers of today's teenagers grew up expecting to be virgins when they married and to stride down the aisle in pristine white gowns that signified their sexual purity. In fact, so great was the pressure to be a virgin that nonvirgins went to great lengths to feign sexual innocence. For example, shortly before a wedding, a woman might have gone to a physician to ask for a "lover's knot": the doctor placed a few stitches in the labia to cause pain and bleeding on the bride's wedding night.[5]

Even today, the notion of the virgin bride is not totally obsolete. In contemporary societies where marriages are sometimes still arranged by parents, such as in Iran and India, virginity remains a requisite for marriage.

In 1994, the median age for first marriages was between 25 and 27 years of age.[6] By then, young women have probably dated for many years, leaving few with their virginity by the time they take their marriage vows. By age 26, in fact, only 1 in 50 Americans is a virgin.[7]

Given the sophistication and sexual experience of teenagers today, is virginity truly evidence of sexual innocence? After all, many virgins have indulged in a considerable amount of necking, petting, and other kinds of intimate sexual behavior. (Too, many nonvirgins who have had sexual intercourse a few times do not consider themselves sexual sophisticates.)

While there may be less emphasis on adhering to a "virgin until marriage" code, the idea of aspiring to postpone sexual initiation, at least until there is a suitable partner and the young person feels ready, persists. Many people strive to remain virgins for as long as possible, especially religious youth.

At a 1993 convention sponsored by the Southern Baptists, a seventeen-year-old male took a pledge of sexual abstinence until marriage. "I want to give that as a gift to my wife. I want it to be special, not something I do just to fit in."[8] Hundreds of other teenagers have signed similar pledges of purity and gone public with their vow to remain chaste.

Students at Philadelphia Girls High, in Philadelphia, Pennsylvania, formed a Virgins Club, which meets once a week after school.[9] At these meetings, over seventy-five high school students join in discussions of sexual issues. "As a member of this club," explained one girl, "we're saying virgin is not a bad word and that it's OK to be one. We date," she added. "We go out with male friends. But we know who to go with and how far we will go."[10]

Not everyone chooses to make public statements about their virginity, nor makes a deliberate decision to preserve it, particularly not young males. As another member of the Philadelphia Girls High club observed, "There are a lot of guy virgins out there. But unless they're into religion, they don't want anybody to know it, trend or no trend. In fact, many guys may even lie about it."[11]

WHAT'S ALL THE FUSS?

Why is there—to this day—so much attention paid to the issue of virginity? And why do so many sex curricula stress virginity as the only option for teenagers?

First, many religious persons regard nonmarital sexual intercourse as sinful and detrimental to marriage. According to Christian theologian Wesley Granby, reserving intercourse for marriage ensures that any "ghosts of partners past cannot erode the confidence two people have in their sexual performance."[12] When both partners are virgins, they cannot compare or be compared to former partners, giving them more confidence and security to grow together in sexual experience.

Besides religious reasons, there are practical ones. As in days past, virginity can protect a person against getting a bad reputation. But more importantly, it frees a woman from worrying about missed periods or positive pregnancy test results. And although it isn't a blanket guarantee, *virginity protects against sexually transmitted diseases.*

Emotionally, virginity has other benefits. Learning to control sexual urges is a challenge. Those who meet that challenge by maintaining their virginity can take pride in having self-control. Whenever we learn to restrain ourselves—whether it is learning to keep our tempers from flaring or to refrain from bad habits, or to restrain our sexual desires—we also gain in temperance (restraint) and moral character.

Furthermore, because virginity frees people from worry about pregnancy and STDs, it helps many young people feel more in control of their personal lives. Appreciating this freedom from worry, and the greater control, many people choose to stay virgins until they are ready to relinquish that freedom and share their sexuality with someone else. As one woman explained, "I felt I lost some power when I lost my virginity because it was the only thing I had of my own that I hadn't shared until that point."[13]

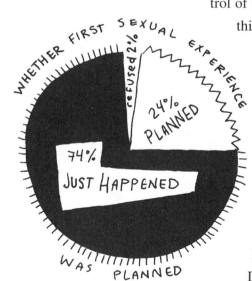

Discovering and experiencing sexual intercourse for the first time, as two virgins do together, can create a unique emotional and spiritual bond that makes postponing sexual initiation worthwhile. Finally, postponing sexual intercourse can actually act as an aphrodisiac (sex tonic), making a relationship more romantic. During the period while a couple is waiting, they can master the skills of foreplay and other sexual acts that deepen and broaden the sexual experience beyond intercourse.

To summarize the "pro-virginity" argument: virginity keeps some people in line with their religions; prevents pregnancy, disease, and bad reputations; helps a person develop self-control; and fosters a unique bonding between two people.

With these advantages, many people think that virginity "has all the answers." But here is what virginity cannot do: It cannot make you a better person, in the sense that it doesn't make you any more thoughtful, kind, or considerate when you do have sex. (It takes more than sexual purity to do that.) Nor can preserving virginity guarantee you a long-lasting marriage, a strong relationship, or a positive initiation into sex. Again, these all require something more.

One woman claimed that her virginity spoiled her wedding day. For, on what should have been a thoroughly joyous day, she worried about how sex was going to be that night, and how much it might hurt.

Many people are eager to have sex, but are so committed to remaining virgins until their wedding day that they rush into marriage unprepared for the emotional commitment that marriage requires. Or, once their curiosity about sex is satiated, they discover that they have made the wrong choice for a lifetime mate; sexual desire clouded their better judgment. If they had engaged in intercourse before their marriage, they might have spared themselves and their spouses the pain of divorce.

Finally, even *if* virginity is desirable, to make it the sole requirement, or the most essential one for choosing a lifelong partner, is foolish. Rejecting an otherwise wonderful person because he or she is not a virgin is akin to throwing the baby out with the bathwater.

LIKE A VIRGIN

What is a virgin anyway? If we limit the definition to someone who has not engaged in heterosexual intercourse, then a person can be a virgin even with a background of heavy petting, mutual masturbation, and oral or anal sex. This narrow definition diminishes the importance of sexual satisfaction that is attained by means other than vaginal/penile intercourse.

Karen Bouris, author of *The First Time*, a book about female sexual awakening, urges us to consider the issue of virginity in the light of history. In the past, virgins had distinct advantages that nonvirgins did not. Virgins had better chances of marrying, and they avoided the scandal of illegitimate births. But today, Bouris notes, "Women have far more than their virginity with which to measure their worth to others and to themselves."[14]

The term "losing (your) virginity" is troubling because it implies something lost, or given away. As one person said, "I don't feel as though we really lose anything. I feel we gain a better understanding of ourselves and our bodies; knowledge about sex and sexuality; and a greater amount of self-confidence."[15] And as another commented, "Sometimes I wonder if 'when, where, and with whom' you lost your virginity is important at all. I would rather talk about who was my first true love or the first time I enjoyed having a sexual relationship . . . not the one night I lost my virginity."[16]

When virginity is perceived as a loss, especially if lost through incest, date rape, or other sexually abusive conduct, young people may erroneously conclude that their "goodness" or virtue can never be regained. Yet, if one puts less value on virginity and its "loss," it becomes easier to value others for who they are—not for what has happened to them.

Virginity does mean a loss of sexual innocence, which cannot be restored. However, it is *never too late to abstain from sex until you are ready for it. Nor is it ever too late to find the right person, with whom having sex will make up for any previous disappointments.*

Further, the idea that the loss of virginity is a *milestone* event creates a heavy burden of expectations. Many skills take time and experience to learn; so does sex. If you consider the first time as a beginning, not a loss, then you can gain a healthier perspective. The quality of first-time sexual experiences should never be used to gauge what you can eventually learn and experience. Sex improves as people learn what pleases themselves and their partners—something that takes years, not moments, to achieve.

FOR THE RIGHT REASONS

In the real, not-always-so-moral, world, some people use sex to barter for popularity, affection, and even money, jobs, or other gains. Just as it is wrong to use sex in this way, it is also wrong to use virginity as a bartering tool. Virginity or the lack of virginity does not make a person good or bad. Many people had no choice in becoming a nonvirgin, while others are virgins not because of a moral commitment but because of a lack of opportunity.

Additionally, intercourse is not the be-all and end-all of sex. Kissing, fondling, and close dancing can be sexually gratifying and can bond two people together—with fewer risks, hassles, or emotional consequences than intercourse.

Again, sexual morality requires freedom, respect, the ability to make wise decisions, and the self-control to restrain sexual urges. Obviously, if preserving virginity is to have any moral merit, it needs to be an intentional, well-considered decision. Conversely, people who lose their sexual purity against their will are not morally culpable (responsible); we are only *morally* responsible for behavior that we choose to do or refrain from doing.

Likewise, moral living means learning from our mistakes. Many young adults say that they wish they had delayed having sexual intercourse until they were more mature or had found more suitable partners or circumstances.[17]

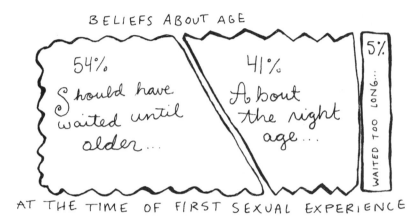

BELIEFS ABOUT AGE

54% Should have waited until older...

41% About the right age...

5% WAITED TOO LONG...

AT THE TIME OF FIRST SEXUAL EXPERIENCE

Waiting for the right time and the right person before engaging in sexual intimacy can be difficult, especially considering that most teenagers will remain single for many years. Even so, erring on the side of caution can never hurt. After all, no one ever died from a lack of sex. And true love waits.

WHEN THE ROAD FORKS

People committed to waiting may face a moral dilemma at times. During wartime, for instance, many couples committed to virginity decide to have intercourse before one of them leaves for battle, where the risk of injury or death are great. Priests and nuns who have taken vows of celibacy occasionally fall in love with someone and face the moral dilemma of breaking those vows.

However wrenching or difficult, these moral dilemmas should not be mistaken for moral confusion. Nor are they all that typical. Many American teenagers make the decision to lose their virginity out of peer pressure, curiosity, or because they believe themselves ready for sexual experience.

Certainly, people who put a high value on maintaining virginity owe it to themselves not to let alcohol cloud their judgment or permit other people to pressure them into compromise. They also deserve to be free of the pressure to conform to standards that they don't share.

If you feel that you had sexual intercourse before you were ready to have it, or if you were forced to have sex, remember that you haven't lost your character. Even people with reputations for much sexual experience have an opportunity to gain from their past. After all, *character is being a good person and knowing who you are, not necessarily who others think you are.* Character also means taking responsibility for your own behavior.

GETTING OFF TO A GOOD START

We live in a diverse society, among people with many different moral compasses and competing moral claims. Making the right decisions requires foresight and wisdom, traits that may come with age and experience.

Often, the choice feels right. But just as often, choosing when to have sexual intercourse can be difficult and confusing, especially when other people besides ourselves are affected by our decisions. Moreover, pressuring someone else to make a decision against their own beliefs denies them the autonomy they deserve.

We have all seen self-righteous people who believe that they have

93

a monopoly on moral truth, and are intolerant of any viewpoint that differs from their own, especially on an issue like virginity. Many times, conflicts arise between parents who insist that their children re-

main virgins and children who believe that they have a right to make that decision themselves.

The decision to have intercourse should be a mature, conscious choice. Try to be sure that when you decide you are ready for sexual intimacy, you are acting freely, without coercion or guilt. Responsible people will think about birth control and disease prevention beforehand.

Although many people are quite certain about virginity and its place in their moral code, others are not quite sure whether it is an outdated custom, a practical guide, or an ideal. Regardless of when they decide to gain sexual experience, including after marriage, people need to understand that a *satisfying sex life does not necessarily require that every time we have sex, it is good sex—even the first time.*

Finally, when virginity is not regarded as a major pivotal experience (or loss), then a person may have other opportunities through the course of a lifetime to have a positive sexual awakening.

9

TO TELL THE TRUTH

Alison wasn't feeling well, so she went to her family doctor. After diagnosing a bladder infection, Dr. Blakely asked her, directly, "Are you sleeping with your boyfriend?" (Bladder infections commonly occur when girls first start having sexual intercourse.)

Alison was dumbfounded by the question and perplexed about how to answer it. She had started having sex with her boyfriend, and was worried that if she answered truthfully, Dr. Blakely would tell her mother. And the last person she wanted informed about her sex life was her mother because she and her mother had very different opinions about the issue.

Although Dr. Blakely assured Alison that what she told him would remain confidential, she feared otherwise, remembering that her friend Lucy had gone to a clinic for an abortion and the abortion counselor had notified Lucy's parents.

That night Alison wrote in her diary about how weird it felt telling Dr. Blakely about her private life, and that she didn't think it was anybody's business except her own. Soon Alison recovered from her bladder infection and put the incident on a back burner while she diligently studied for spring exams. Then, early one evening, Alison's mother marched into her room, demanding to know if Alison was sleeping with Ted (her boyfriend).

To Alison's horror, her mother was clutching her diary, insisting that Alison confess—although clearly she had already read about her daughter's activities in the diary. Alison's thoughts rushed back to Dr. Blakely. Had he broken his promise and squealed on Alison? Or, did Alison's mother grow suspicious after she caught Alison lying on the sofa with Ted as they watched a video, their legs intertwined? (Her mother was constantly warning Alison not to get too intimate with Ted.)

No matter what the cause, Alison's mother had searched through Alison's room, read her private writing, and was now screaming at her. Indignant over the invasion of her privacy and her mother's accusations, Alison stormed past her mother, bolted down the stairs, and charged out the door.

Her mother followed her to the driveway and stood there, alternately shouting and crying, as Alison pedaled off down the street on her bicycle, her mind racing as fast as her feet were pedaling. What business did her mother have snooping through her room and reading her diary?

Did she really think that she could stop Alison from having sex with Ted? Oh, she made it difficult for Alison to get birth control. And she made it clear that she thought such behavior was sinful, wrong, and dangerous. At seventeen, though, Alison thought that she was entitled to make decisions about her sexual behavior with a measure of privacy, and she certainly did not expect to have to defend herself as though she were on trial.

True, if Alison ever found herself pregnant or sick, the responsibility for her care, and perhaps that of an infant, would no doubt be shared by her mother. Knowing how much her mother disapproved of her having sex with her boyfriend, Alison hid the truth from her. She also hid her birth control pills, and lied to her mother when she and Ted were at his house while his parents were away at work. She pretended she was going to the library or the mall, and because her mother trusted her, Alison's ruse had always worked. Still, she would occasionally ask her older sister to cover up for her, in case her mother did question Alison's whereabouts.

Although the names in this story have been changed, it is a true story. It is also a common one, which occurs in many homes where parents discourage and disapprove of intimate sexual activity, and their adolescent children engage in such behavior.

Most teenagers assume that their sexual behavior is their own private business. And some parents respect that privacy. Yet many parents do not. Even the law is divided on the subject. In some states, adolescents are entitled to keep information about their sexual behavior private, while in other states teens cannot get birth control requiring medical assistance, such as diaphragms or Norplant, be treated for sexually transmitted diseases, or obtain an abortion without parental consent.[1]

Some states don't require consent, but do require that parents be notified. In a few states, parental consent or notification extends to noncustodial parents, including those who have been absent from a child's life for a long time.[2]

Whether or not parents have a right to deny their teenagers access to birth control or abortion is an important issue. The immediate issue Alison and teenagers like her face, though, is one of truthfulness. How much truthfulness is it fair to expect or demand from a teenager? Does her mother have a right to know about Alison's sexual behavior, including what birth control she uses, or if Alison is pregnant, and if she seeks an abortion? And what means does she have a right to use to obtain that information? In turn, what duty does Alison have to be truthful to her mother and what right does she have to withhold the truth from her parents, as well as from future boyfriends, or anyone else?

To reveal or withhold the truth vexes nearly everyone at some time or another. Keeping truly painful experiences (such as incest or rape) secret can interfere with the healing process. Secrets can also distance us from people with whom we are trying to establish a close bond. On the other hand, candor and confessions can cause undeserved pain to the confessor or the person who hears the secret. Yet they can also bring emotional intimacy, compassion, and understanding to a friendship or relationship.

A DOUBLE-EDGED SWORD

Two best friends, Heidi and Danielle, make dinner for their boyfriends. When Heidi's boyfriend, Garth, plants a sensual kiss on Danielle's mouth and whispers in her ear about how hot she is, Danielle laughs off the incident. What a flirt, she thinks.

A few nights later, Garth drops in on Danielle. Aware that she might be doing something wrong, she nonetheless feels remarkably excited to walk such a moral precipice. When Garth starts kissing her again, she is confused, but goes along with him.

Afterward, overcome with guilt and remorse, Danielle pleads

with Garth to keep their little tryst a secret from Heidi. Yet what if Garth tells Heidi anyway? What if Garth never tells Heidi and eventually marries her, as the two have planned? Does Danielle have an obligation to her friend to reveal what has occured? After all, if he came on to Danielle, he might be fooling around with some other girls, too. Or, if nothing is said of the incident, won't Heidi be spared the pain of betrayal?

Lying to keep a matter private may be motivated by a wish to avoid pain or rejection. For example, James was treated for childhood cancer and was left sterile, a condition with which he is still trying to come to terms. Since James is only in high school and unready for either parenting or marriage, does he have any obligation to tell anyone he dates about his condition? If so, at what point does that obligation begin?

Does a girl have an obligation to tell her boyfriend that she has had breast-reduction surgery or any other plastic surgery? Must people reveal that they are fearful of sex or that their sexual interests are unconventional? For instance, Maria, who is outgoing and vivacious, gets a lot of attention from guys. Yet Maria has no interest in them, only in other females. Does she have any obligation to curtail their interest in her?

Sometimes the obligation to reveal a secret is obvious: The conflict centers on how and when. Millions of Americans are infected with the herpes virus, for which there is limited treatment and no known cure. Debbie is one of those people. Although she feels obligated to tell prospective sexual partners about her condition, her moral dilemma is when, and how, to do it.

Should Debbie tell a date right away, thereby giving him a chance to avoid any emotional entanglement if he can't or doesn't want to deal with her genital herpes? Is it fair to Debbie, though, to be judged so early, when someone might work harder at finding a way to deal with her problem *after* he makes an emotional commitment to her?

Finally, secrets can be a double-edged sword. Carmen and Ryan have been friends all year; they talk almost daily. Lately, though, Carmen finds that she is increasingly attracted to Ryan—not just as a friend, but romantically. If she tells this to Ryan, she knows that it may make him feel uncomfortable and possibly ruin their easygoing friendship. On the other hand, Carmen wonders if Ryan feels the same way toward her, and that perhaps by putting the issue out in the open, they could be more honest about their feelings.

IN THE NAME OF VIRTUE

Sometimes, a secret may be clouded with so much emotion that the decision to reveal it is difficult to make. Consider the following situation:

When Joe was little, he was sexually molested by his uncle. At the time he was too scared and embarrassed to tell anyone about it. Lately, though, Joe has been getting help. Coincidentally, around the same time Joe began seeing a counselor, his uncle started going to AA meetings, and appeared to be trying to straighten himself out. Does Joe have a right or a duty to confront his uncle or tell his uncle's family about the molestation? After all, his uncle's behavior may have been related to his alcohol abuse and he may have overcome his problem. On the other hand, he may also have molested other children, who could benefit by the disclosure.

Many people argue that the end justifies the means. But does it? Traditionally, the names of women who are sexually active or easily seduced (or who aren't, but someone wants to say that they are) have been scrawled on the walls of men's rooms, where the women had no way of refuting the claims, or cleaning up their reputations—literally.

Women have recently adopted this tradition, but they scrawl the names of suspected or known rapists. Assuming that the men are guilty, does such vigilantism live up to our moral principles?

KEEPING SECRETS

According to Marty Klein, therapist and author of *Your Sexual Secrets*, most of us have sexual secrets we intend to keep forever, or at least from our current sexual partners. The most common of these secrets are sexual pasts, sexual fantasies, fears, and the like.[3]

Nearly half of all states have some kind of notification laws compelling women who are pregnant to inform their sexual partner (or pregnant minors to inform their parents). Even in the absence of such laws, what right does a pregnant woman have to keep her condition secret from her partner?

Resolving this dilemma, where different people have different moral claims, is exceedingly difficult. One guideline is to judge who has the greatest moral claim. In this case it is the woman, because she will experience all the physical consequences of pregnancy, as well as the emotional ones. However, some people go by the rule that *any* party who can make a moral claim has a right to be notified. Following this reasoning, a woman would have a duty to tell the man who impregnated her, especially if she is considering having the baby and keeping it, since the man would (or should) share the emotional and economical responsibility. Similarly, since her parents have a vested interest in the welfare of their daughter, they, too, may have a right to know.

Which rule is correct does not vary from person to person; it's just that because the situation is so difficult to figure out—the truth, so to speak, so complicated to understand—that ethicists, policymakers, and people in general cannot agree which rule is the right one. This is what makes such decisions so complicated, but so necessary. Because laws and customs affect millions of people, they do not always reflect moral truth.

A PROTECTIVE SHIELD

"Secrecy may be used to guard intimacy or invade," says ethicist Sissela Bok, author of *Secrets*, "to nurture or consume it."[4]

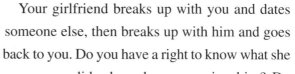

Your girlfriend breaks up with you and dates someone else, then breaks up with him and goes back to you. Do you have a right to know what she did when she was seeing him? Do you have a right to even ask her?

What right do you have to know about a partner's first sexual experience or sexual history? If you are dating a person a friend has dated, do you have a right to ask your friend to tell you what that person is like sexually?

Again, the answers to these questions pose a moral conflict for many people. Telling each other a secret can bond people together and help them understand each other. Yet many people feel more emotionally secure keeping a part of themselves private. They also want to guard their sexual history from other people, especially if they are not deeply committed to those people. If we use as a moral guidepost the basic principle of treating people kindly, the question becomes less vexing and clearer to answer.

Keeping a secret can be difficult, especially if someone asks you to keep the secret before telling you what it is they are pledging you to keep secret! How much right does a person have to expect you to keep a secret? For example, what if a friend makes you promise to keep a secret and then tells you that she is pregnant? After five months, you feel that you should tell someone because your friend is not getting any medical care (despite your efforts to convince her she should). On the other hand, you know it would hurt her to be betrayed. In this case, the moral claim of her baby enters the argument, and doing right by the baby might mean betraying your friend and hoping that she will forgive you.

If a person has fathered a child or placed a child up for adoption, does he have the right to keep this information secret? Does anyone have the right to withhold information about his or her virginity or sexual experience? Does anyone have the right to remain silent about an STD that has been cured or is under control?

How much obligation do we have to let others keep their secrets? In fact, what questions do we even have the right to ask? Given the risks of sexually transmitted disease, anyone has the right to ask whether their sexual partner has a disease or engages in behavior that exposes him or her to a disease, including any drug habits. But does that right extend to demanding a test to prove these claims?

A few years ago, Joan ran away from home after her stepfather had sexually abused her. That part of her life is history now, since

Joan's mom divorced her stepfather and Joan returned home and went back to school, choosing a different school where she hoped she could get a fresh start.

What right does Joan have to guard her past? Do individuals who have been raped, molested, or sexually harassed have the right to guard the incident from others, or at least keep their names from public view?

Unlike other crime victims, the identity of rape victims generally is withheld from publication, with the reasoning that their true identity causes a victim further (and perhaps unnecessary) pain. Recently, a few rape victims have voluntarily challenged this practice, and a few publications have published the names of victims. Those who defend the practice argue that by remaining silent about victims' names, they set them apart from victims of other crimes, and actually contribute to keeping the crime a personal disgrace rather than merely a crime.

SEEKING THE TRUTH

"Against every claim to secrecy stands an awareness of its dangers," warns ethicist Sissela Bok, in *Secrets*.[5] Likewise, seeking the truth can be a painful endeavor.

In a highly unusual, albeit provocative, case, a doctor in southern Ohio treated dozens of couples for infertility. Because of their particular medical problems, the women were artifically inseminated with sperm. Instead of seeking anonymous donors, however, the doctor used his own sperm, unbeknownst to his patients. Dozens of unsuspecting women bore children with the doctor's genes. Many of these children live in the same vicinity; their chance of dating and marrying one another, while slim, is still upsetting. What duty is there to test all the children who were born to the doctor's patients, in order to find out if their mothers were victims of the doctor's deception?

Obviously, such cases are the exception, rather than the rule. But having to make a decision about whether or not to ferret out the truth is far more common. Many adoptees wish to search for their biological roots, seeking the truth about their conception and the identities of their biological parents. Do these adoptees have any moral claim to know the circumstances of their conception—whether it occurred during a rape, say, or a casual or paid sexual encounter, or if the biological father is a relative of the mother?

Do birth parents who give children up for adoption have any right to contact those children later? Do siblings have a right to know about brothers or sisters conceived in former or subsequent relationships of one or both of their parents?

Does any teenager have the right to know if he or she: was conceived before his or her parents' betrothal? is the child of an adulterous liaison? was fathered by a sperm donor or conceived by a surrogate mother?

Again, as in so many other moral situations, the moral claims of each party need to be weighed. Many adoptees feel that their lives are the ones most affected by the adoption and the secrecy shrouding their genetic and medical backgrounds. Certainly, though, the privacy of a woman who gave a child up for adoption many years ago has a moral claim. Moreover, *knowledge* of the truth may be one claim; the right to contact and become acquainted, another. Many cultures actually encourage open adoptions and a lack of secrecy, while others, such as our own, discourage the practice and make it difficult to ferret out the truth.

As in so many other moral situations, different customs do not mean that morality is relative. The good of a child in one society and the reasons that would drive a woman to place her child up for adoption may require a certain amount of privacy and secrecy. In another society, such privacy may be unnecessary, unwarranted, and therefore in no need of protection. Regardless, many people believe that adoptees are always entitled to know the truth, but that the privacy rights of biological parents depend on the social climate in which they live and on the circumstances of their lives.

Candor has an important place in sexual relationships. Yet according to both Klein and Bok, secrets have a rightful place, too. Whether or not to tell the truth has no easy answer. Sometimes we only know what is right after we have done the wrong thing!

It helps to remember that those moral decisions that involve a great risk or sacrifice cause a lot of conflict. Also, a moral life requires accepting that we cannot always be certain of the truth; all that we can do is stay committed to the struggle to find it.

10

IN GOOD TASTE

A look at Americans at leisure, at amusement parks and other places in the United States, suggests an easygoing dress code. People wear just about anything, sometimes without underwear, and sometimes underwear as outerwear.

Clothing functions to protect people from extremes in the weather, sunburn, insect bites, and industrial hazards. Ironically, though, one of the primary purposes of clothing is not to serve these functions but to communicate. Just as words, gestures, and body language tell much about people, so does their choice of clothing, or sartorial expression, as that choice is called.

According to Alison Lurie, author of *The Language of Clothing*, clothing can reveal a person's occupation, personality, opinions, current mood, and sexual feelings.[1]

Members of prehistoric societies used clothing to communicate status and sexuality. In necklaces and loincloths, men wore animal teeth and skins to indicate their success and status as hunters. Other tribal members adorned their bodies with paint, jewelry, tattoos, and scars to convey messages of desirability and availability.

In much the same way, contemporary people use clothes, tattoos, and other body adornments to communicate their sexuality. Back in the 1950s, cinema idol James Dean delivered a sexual message through his leather jacket, white T-shirt, and tight jeans. Today, we see women in backless and low-cut clothing, short skirts, open shirts, stretchy, clingy, and sensuous fabrics, navel rings, and more. In the same vein, some men wear tank tops, skintight jeans, and boots that sugggest sex appeal and manliness.

IN GOOD TASTE

Whether the choice of clothing is in good or bad taste depends on the custom and etiquette of a particular society. As fashion shows, these are constantly evolving. Once it was indecent for a woman to show any part of her legs, including her ankles; nowadays, she can attend a formal wedding and nearly bare her legs completely. On the other hand, males are not expected to draw attention to their penises. Centuries ago, however, courtly gentlemen wore codpieces, a fashion item that fit like an athletic cup (and covered the opening in their breeches). Today, anything resembling a codpiece, except perhaps in a dance costume or football uniform, would bring stares and disapproval.

Whether or not clothing has a sexually *moral* component is an altogether different question than that of good taste. For example, topless attire was customary among the natives of Bali and Hawaii. Christian missionaries, whose societies stressed modesty, misread impropriety and sinfulness into the native dress. The missionaries imposed their standards on the natives, urging them to cover up and dress more discreetly.

Dress codes may involve issues of sexual ethics. Do employers have the right to require employees to wear sexually provocative clothing? For example, should waitresses be required to wear fishnet stockings, stiletto-heeled shoes, and skimpy, restrictive corsets in order to keep their jobs? After all, what does such attire have to do with taking an order and bringing a meal?

Gloria Gonzalez suspected that there is a connection. Bored with her secretarial job, Gonzalez decided to be a street vendor and sell hot dogs outside a men's club. Only she chose to sell them clad in a thong bikini. Sure enough, Gonzalez had terrific sales. What was not terrific, though, was that the Florida state law regarded her attire as indecent exposure. As a result, Gonzalez was arrested.

Andrew Martinez wore even less than a bikini. With the exception of a backpack slung over his shoulders and a pair of sandals on his feet, the twenty-year-old anthropology student at the University of California at Berkeley wore nothing on campus. "Clothes are totally a creation of need and capitalistic society," reasoned Martinez, better known as the Naked Guy. Campus officials did not warm up to

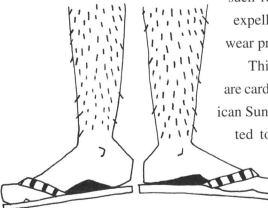

such reasoning, however, and soon expelled Martinez for his "failure to wear proper attire."[2]

Thirty-five thousand Amerians are card-carrying nudists of the American Sunbathing Association, committed to bathing nude and bowling nude.[3] Although there are no federal laws prohibiting nudity, many local ordinances outlaw it and many people are offended by it.

Why do naked bodies, nudists ask, offend so many Americans? And why is it always associated with sexual immorality? "One nude draped on a settee in a dimly lit room may be sexy," observed Jane and Michael Stern, two journalists writing a piece on nudist camps, "but a hundred nudes standing in line for tuna salad at high noon in the mess hall are anything but."[4]

While public nudity remains outside popular custom, going topless is acceptable—at least for men in American society. Ever since a change in state law in 1936, New York City men have been permitted to go shirtless in public. From construction workers and landscapers to bikers and sunbathers, men routinely shed their shirts.

With their well-developed pectorals and biceps, many of these men look sexy. However, no matter how sexy they look, none are denied the right to go topless in public. Women are not accorded the same right. For as sexy as the men look, women would be considered even sexier going topless. Is the distinction fair?

Is there any logic to dress codes that compel waitresses to wear provocative outfits, allow men to go shirtless, but prevent women from breastfeeding their infants in public? In 1993, the New York State legislature finally passed an exception to its obscenity bill, allowing women to nurse their babies in public.[5] Many women did not think that they should need a law to protect what they believed was a natural right to nurse wherever and whenever. But women do not have universal protection, nor does everyone consider nursing in public a natural right. By 1994, only three states had passed similar statutes.[6]

In a Vermont library, one sign reads No Eating or Breastfeeding. Even if so many Americans are uneasy about seeing a real nipple used in a nonsexual way, do they have the right to impose their prudery on others, especially hungry babies? Mary Lou Schloss, spokesperson for the Coalition for Topfree Equality, suggests that if women were allowed to routinely go topless, the sexiness of topless women would diminish. This, in turn, would allow women to "more comfortably and easily make the decision to nurse a baby in public."[7]

Other dress codes are also difficult to understand. Do schools have the right to insist that females wear bras and keep their midriffs covered? Do they have any right to make male students shave, remove their earrings, or refrain from wearing skintight pants?

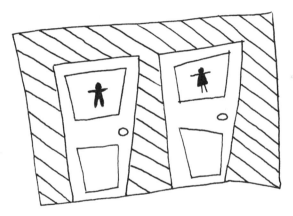

Denise Wells was fined $200 for using a men's rest room when the waiting line at the women's rest room was too long.[8] Was that fair? If women are allowed in the men's rooms, should men be allowed in the women's rooms? Or, are unisex rest rooms fairer than gender-segregated ones?

Should prostitutes be allowed to hawk their wares in public?

Is it right to use sex to sell asexual products?

Is sex on afternoon television, when many children are home alone, appropriate or right?

A new bed-and-breakfast business was started in a small midwestern town, serving champagne breakfast in bed by a tuxedoed waiter. Apparently, the enterprise offended a local minister, who led a campaign to close the business, claiming that it undermined the moral values of his community. Did it? Do private citizens have the right to keep topless bars, swinging bars, and singles bars out of their neighborhoods? Does the presence of such establishments erode sexual standards? Or, does it merely mirror them? Indeed, does the public, the government, or any interest group have a right to censor immodesty, nudity, or public displays of affection?

Do couples strolling through school halls have any moral responsibility to contain their passion or keep it private? Is "groping" in public wrong?

Does a couple owe others with them any responsibility to refrain from kissing, necking, or petting? For example, should Heather and Justin, who have been together for over a year, refrain from engaging in any sexual activity in front of Cara and Matt, who are on their first date?

THERE'S NO PLACE LIKE HOME

The majority of sexully active young people customarily have sex at home—theirs, their partners, or someone else's home. The rest have sex in a car or "somewhere else."[9]

While there is no place like home, home turf also may include certain moral conflicts and dilemmas.

One of the most difficult tasks for parents is to help their children develop character—and to allow their children to think and act for themselves. If children are allowed to think for themselves, however, and make independent moral choices, they will not always agree with everything their parents believe to be right. Still, family life requires mutual respect.

Moreover, given the possible consequences of some actions—such as pregnancy and disease—parents may have certain moral claims. Parents also recognize that what may be innocent and private behavior, such as necking, can lead to behavior that has serious consequences. And even though they wish to be home to chaperone their children, many parents regrettably cannot.

Given those circumstances, how much should parents be able to trust their children to conform to their standards? And when are their demands unreasonable?

Many parents, for example, disapprove of heavy petting or nonmarital intercourse, and consequently forbid such behavior. Do the children of these parents have any moral obligation to respect their parents' wishes, if only in their parents' home?

Actually, knowing that they are engaging in forbidden behavior inspires many teenagers to defy their parents and risk getting caught (by disapproving or angry parents). And many teens reason that having sex in the safety of someone's home is worth the risk of getting caught. However, just as consent is essential between two sexual partners, respecting a partner's relationship with his or her parents is also essential. That means refraining from pressuring them into behavior that would immeasurably strain relations between them and their parents.

Frank likes to show off his physique and parade around his home wearing only briefs. His sister is less enthusiastic about Frank's habit, particularly when her friends visit. True, home should be a place where we can relax and be ourselves. Nonetheless, what obligation does Frank have to his sister to be more discreet around her friends?

Do younger brothers and sisters have any moral claims, such as protection from sexual activity they may misunderstand, such as loud sounds or grunts? Is it right or wrong to ask younger siblings to cover for you and lie about your whereabouts and sexual activities? Is it right to teach them sexual behavior, such as masturbation, that your parents might not want them taught?

Because it defies convention or good taste, having sex in certain places appeals to, and even heightens, the sexuality of some people. Necking in a cemetary, for example, appeals to some people precisely because it feels sacrilegious or disrespectful to do so. Just the *thought* of having sex in a taboo place, such as a public rest room, turns on some people. Where does bad taste cross over into immorality? For instance, if a date's kiss or discreet fondling is acceptable in a movie theater, why is fondling your own body parts taboo there?

Remember the distinction between custom, etiquette, and morality: Custom is what is generally acceptable. Etiquette refers to behavior that doesn't offend people. Morality is choosing right from wrong.[10]

Fashion can add to our sex appeal, as well as diminish it. For example, before it was fashionable to wear tights, they were considered sexy. When they became so fashionable that they appeared everywhere and on nearly every kind of body, they lost some of their sex appeal. Likewise, defying a customary fashion can send a clear sexual message. When it is unfashionable and uncustomary to wear fishnet hosiery to work, defying custom to do so renders them sexier.

Even if people dress in a sexy way, that doesn't mean that they are asking for or deserve to be sexually harassed or abused. (It can, however, mean that they ought to use more common sense.)

Good taste can never misserve a person, while bad taste can easily be misinterpreted as wrongful behavior. And while we could be mindful of what is both customary and tasteful, we can also be mindful of the difference between right and wrong.

11

HOLDING UP YOUR END OF THE DEAL

Gretchen went to a party with a group of friends. There she met a guy from another town, Brad, who thought Gretchen was "pretty hot." Brad liked the way Gretchen danced. He liked the way she looked directly at him when she spoke. He liked her outgoing personality. And by the end of the evening, he liked kissing her.

"I'll call you soon," he promised.

"Sure," Gretchen muttered under her breath. Given her experience, she suspected that Brad was just offering a hollow promise, no more real than the empty practice of asking someone how they are and not listening to the answer.

LITTLE WHITE LIES

"How do I look?" *Terrible, as though you've been through a hurricane.* "Fine, you look just fine."

"Wanna go to the movies tonight?" *Are you for real?*

I wouldn't be caught dead with a dork like you. "I'd love to, but I've already made plans."

Etiquette and custom teach us to tell such "white lies." In fact, good manners and consideration often require them. What moral obligation does any kind of sexual encounter require? Does kissing or other sexual activity carry with it a duty to call again, to care again, or to make good on the promises expressed in the heat of passion?

If a couple has been physically intimate, does that entitle either party to a greater measure of respect and attention? Likewise, does a deep emotional relationship carry with it any duty to engage in physical intimacy or sexual experimentation? At what point, if any, does a relationship require sexual fidelity?

One of the most basic moral principles is *not to hurt others as we would not want to be hurt by them.* Certainly,  learning to refrain from making hollow promises can add to a person's character. Even when a partner is asking for more than we can deliver, we can at least treat that person with kindness and civility.

The traditional double standard and anything-goes moral compasses—"love 'em and leave 'em" and "all's fair in love and war"—gave men, in particular, the license to vanish after sex. Men operating under this reasoning often had brief flings and abandoned their partners, who may have found themselves dealing with an unwanted pregnancy. How can such behavior and lack of concern ever be morally justifiable?

It is easy to look with scorn or disgust at men who use women to satisfy their sexual needs with little regard for their feelings or welfare. Today, though, with more freedom, independence, and equality, some women are also using men for sexual gratification, and later hurting them with abandonment and hollow promises. Yet neither numbers nor custom ever makes such behavior right.

HOLDING UP YOUR END OF THE DEAL

In an advice column several years ago, a columnist asked her female readers what they wanted most from their partners. Overwhelmingly, her readers replied that what they wanted most was to cuddle and feel loved, that such affection was far more important than sexual intimacy or intercourse.

"Just say no" may be the hallmark of sexual responsibility in the shadow of disease and teenage pregnancy. How responsible, though, is saying no to many other forms of sexual behavior, from hand holding and caressing to alternatives to sexual intercourse?

Michael is relaxing, spending the evening with Wendy, watching an old movie on television. No homework to do. No minor spat or serious discord. He is simply not in the mood for cuddling. And Wendy, his girlfriend of three months, is. "Come on, Michael," she tenderly says, snuggling up to him. "Turn off the TV and show me some affection."

Does Michael have a moral obligation to honor Wendy's request? Many people would argue that he does not, that sex is something you do only when you are in the mood. Further, they would argue, you do only what you believe is right to do.

Others disagree, and claim that for the sake of the relationship, Michael ought to show Wendy some physical affection, not necessarily the kind of sex that gets scripted into passionate love scenes, perhaps just some kissing and hugging. Still others believe that if Michael and Wendy were already in a physical relationship, perhaps married to one another, then Michael should let himself get aroused and really enjoy sex with Wendy.

Relationships involve two people, each with the potential for a different sex drive, different attitudes toward sex, and a different set of sexual moral standards. How much right do we have to expect our partner to engage in sex, even just hand holding, cuddling, and kissing, if that individual isn't very physically demonstrative, or at times doesn't feel like it?

We often listen to problems when we'd rather do something else, help with homework, put up with bothersome friends, family, and pets, and make a host of other sacrifices in a relationship with someone we love or care deeply about. Is physical affection or sex so different from these other activities that it should stand alone and be reserved for only those times when the "mood" is right?

How much right do we have to expect more kissing, hand holding, massages, passion, or public displays of affection from our partners than they usually give? What if one person is more sexually adventurous than the other? Which partner's wishes are honored? Does it depend on the type of sexual activity involved? Or, assuming there is no physical risk or harm involved, should a person be willing to experiment, if only once?

Some partners need a great deal of privacy before they feel comfortable with any sexual expression, including kissing. Others need a long time in a relationship before they feel secure about having any kind of physical intimacy. In such relationships, which partner's feelings should be honored? How often is it fair to defer to the person who is less secure about their sexuality? Is it fair to end a relationship on the basis of incompatibility, or is there a moral obligation to work out the differences? What obligation does either partner have to discuss any sexual incompatibility or the reasons behind it?

118

Many young people feel pressured to conform to a certain level of activity, often unaware that hugging or hand holding is not only a fair substitute for physical intimacy but sometimes a preferable one. One high school freshman who had a herpes sore on his lip, solved the good-night-kiss dilemma by hugging his date at the door.

Is a partner entitled to more sex than he or she gets? Is a partner under any obligation to overcome an inhibition? Or the reverse—to become more prudent and modest about sex? What rights does a person have when he or she is together with someone who is intentionally abstaining from sex, or who can't have sex? Although a person has a legal right to end an unconsummated marriage (one where no intercourse has taken place), does he or she have any *moral* right to maintain the marriage and seek sexual satisfaction outside the relationship?

Everyone has a right to *ask* for sex in an intimate relationship, but how often? Over and over again, or just occasionally? At what point would a person be making a nuisance out of him- or herself or crossing over the border of common decency in the way they ask? How much right do we have to turn down a request from someone we are already involved with and how much obligation do we have to accept one?

Does a person have any obligation to do anything about their appearance? Like many other young people, Shannon loved to experiment with her image. After she started dating Tony, she decided to dye her hair a bright color and stop shaving her underarms and legs. "If you love me," she told her boyfriend, "you will love me as I am." Yet try as he did, Tony had a hard time seeing the "new" Shannon in the old, affectionate light. What responsibility to each other and their relationship did each one have to accommodate the other person's expectations?

The answers to these myriad questions are not easy to find, for they lie somewhere between being true to oneself and being selfless toward one's partner. Such give-and-take, though, forms the cornerstone of all relationships, and of how we learn to be better people. Asking the questions is a first step, because it shows recognition that it is not always fair to hold back in a relationship. Indeed, it is partially through sexual activity that we can express our feelings toward another person and show how much we care. Likewise, it is through their willingness to meet our needs, even when they don't feel "up for it," that we can feel more secure and loved.

We all feel that doing something sexual against our will is wrong. At issue here is not sexual activity that is dangerous, distasteful, dishonest, or coerced. Rather, it is sexual behavior that stretches a person's boundaries for the sake of a relationship.

CUTTING SOME SLACK

Julia and Martin kissed for the first time. In fact, it was Martin's first intimate kiss, and he hadn't quite mastered the skill. Julia had always admired Martin's ease with people and his great dancing, so she was somewhat surprised to discover his sexual awkwardness and inexperience.

It is hard to blame someone for being turned off by a sloppy kiss. On the other hand, Martin was a decent person who had treated Julia with respect. Thus, when he called Julia for a second date, he was astonished, disappointed, and hurt when she turned him down.

Did Martin deserve a second chance with Julia? There may be a virtue to cutting people like Martin some slack, but is there any moral obligation to do so?

If someone is withdrawn, shy, or uncomfortable with his or her sexuality, is there any *duty* to be patient, understanding, and kind? If someone has been taught to fear or loathe sexuality, what duty, if any, is there to be tolerant of that viewpoint and to try to help the person think about his or her attitudes about sex?

Here, too, individuals have no duty (nor is there any virtue) to engage in sex with someone who isn't appealing to them. On the other hand, a behavior like kissing is partly a skill. Not wanting to kiss someone who has hurt your feelings is quite different from not wanting to kiss someone because he or she doesn't know how you like to kiss. Although it means going out on a limb and risking hurting someone's pride, telling (or showing) that person how to improve his or her sexual behavior in a tactful way can be helpful to both of you. And investing in a relationship in this way prepares young people for the kind of give-and-take that long-term adult relationships require.

Many disabled people cannot experience a full range of sexual activity. Yet they can learn to compensate in other ways that are sexually gratifying.[1] And for both moral and practical reasons, many teenagers (and adults) choose to refrain from sexual intercourse. Here, too, there are other ways of having sexual experiences. A kiss, a hug, and a massage are all sexual, and can bond people together, as well as prepare them for a time when more intimate sex is appropriate.

BROKEN PROMISES

The beginning of most relationships is usually full of promise—the promise of good times, caring, sharing, and for many, the promise of love. While few teenagers marry and take formal vows to stay together, many teenagers agree (or it is tacitly implied) to remain faithful to each other and refrain from dating anyone else as long as their relationship continues.

Often though, for many of the same reasons that adults stray from their marriage vows, teenage partners break their promise not to date anyone else. This may be a one-time or occasional occurrence, at a party or on a vacation, for instance. Or it may involve an entirely separate relationship on the side.

Unlike marital infidelity, there are no laws against teenage infidelity (unfaithfulness). There are, however, both moral and practical issues, particularly for couples who are sexually active. According to recent findings published in *Sex in America*, the people most likely to get a sexually transmitted disease share one characteristic: They have many sex partners.[2] And if they rarely use condoms, they have ten times the chance of becoming infected with a sexually transmitted disease as someone with few or only one partner.[3] Moreover, the same study revealed that the more sexual partners a person had, the more likely he or she was to have had relationships that were nonexclusive.[4]

Risk of disease is certainly reason enough to stay faithful to one partner. But many teenagers in relationships refrain from sexual intercourse or intimate sexual behavior that can spread disease or result in pregnancy. Even in these relationships, however, there are reasons to remain faithful.

The same basic moral principle of treating people fairly and kindly applies to promises to be true to them. After all, betrayal is hurtful, deceitful, and humiliating to the person betrayed. If a relationship is so troublesome that it drives a person, for whatever reason, to look elsewhere for companionship, then it is exceedingly more honest to deal with the issues directly instead of skirting them by seeing someone else. If that is not possible, then the promise to remain exclusive should end, or the relationship should end altogether. Like many situations in life, though, it is often easier to *strive* for such moral ideals than to actually achieve such behavior!

Many teens get involved with someone else when they wish to avoid the pain of acknowledging that their relationship is hurting. Others find themselves cheating on their promise to remain faithful if their partner has moved, gone away to school, or joined the military. Others succumb to the temptation when someone "comes on" to them, looking and acting too irresistible to pass up. Still others, fearful of being left with no partner, look for someone else before they find the courage to break up with their current boy- or girlfriend.

A few people reason that an outside fling can keep the spark glowing within a relationship. Some use a double standard, reasoning that if a partner isn't ready for sexual intimacy, they have the right to seek sexual gratification outside the relationship. Or they reason that "variety is the spice of life," that they are entitled to cheat on their partner. But does such reasoning or behavior pass the reality test? Deception rarely serves to strengthen a bond, and in many cases, a lack of trust (or pattern of lying) contributes to its demise.

Many teenagers bring different expectations to a relationship. Some people are uncomfortable or reluctant to talk about the terms of their relationship and what exactly is expected of them. "We need to have a talk" is often met with "Why does she (or he) need to spell everything out all the time?" Perhaps, though, a reluctance to be clear about faithfulness is actually a reluctance or an unreadiness to make a commitment to just one person. One person may be in love and want to make a commitment. In contrast, the partner may be ambivalent about his or her feelings and unwilling or unready to be tied down or to promise to be faithful. These disparate feelings lead to different expectations. If a couple cannot communicate clearly or reach an agreement or compromise, then the partner who is unwilling to commit exclusively may *appear* to be philandering when in reality he or she has never promised to be faithful.

Another common situation among teenagers (and adults) is the triangle—Beth, Jason, and Jodi, for example. Beth and Jason have been a couple for a year, and Jodi is a good friend of theirs. Suddenly, Jodi finds herself attracted to Jason in a romantic way. Should she tell Jason about her feelings and does she have a right to try to lure him away from Beth?

Fairness to Beth would deny Jodi a right to contribute to the breakup of Beth and Jason. Others would argue that if Jodi were friendly with only Jason, she would have the right to lure him away, reasoning that if Jodi *could* come between Beth and Jason, then the relationship was destined to end anyway.

Just as it does in marriage, though, the promise to remain faithful protects a couple after the initial infatuation wears off and quieter love has settled in. Philosopher Michael Wreen argues that adultery (unfaithfulness in marriage) is wrong because it is so inconsistent with our basic definition of marriage—the agreement to make an emotional commitment to another person, have a sexual relationship with him or her, and have it be *exclusive of anyone else*. In his opinion, the very value of marriage makes monogamy a worthwhile sacrifice.[5] The same rationale can be applied to teenage romance, that a promise to be faithful protects the relationship and allows it to grow without the threat of interference.

There was a time when people who dated either went steady or "dated around." Both were acceptable and the norm. Today, perhaps in part because so many more high school students are sexually active, that norm has been replaced by a new one—young people promise to commit to a relationship early, after only a few dates. While some of these couples stay together for a long time, most teenage romances are rather short, enduring sometimes only weeks or months. If there is a clear, mutual understanding or a promise to be faithful as long as the relationship lasts, then each person has an obligation to fulfill their commitment. If they can't, they have a duty to change the terms of the relationship in an open, honest manner.

Mark and Sharon had dated for nearly two years and remained faithful to each other after Mark went away to college. Then, he decided that as much as he loved Sharon, he needed to spread his wings before settling down with just one person. Sharon was disappointed and scared about losing Mark, but she appreciated his honesty. Perhaps he would find someone else he loved better (and he knew that he faced the same risk). Still, Mark's honesty spared Sharon the humiliation of deceit, gave her an informed choice about whether or not she wanted to remain sexually active with Mark, who might now have sex with someone else, and protected the friendship they still had the opportunity to maintain. (They also had the choice of going separate ways.)

Teenage romances are not expected to last for a lifetime (though a few do). Despite that limitation, however, teens can decide on the terms they want or can deliver, much the way they need to consider

125

the issue of consent. When you can't make a commitment, don't let yourself be coerced into one. And when you can no longer keep your promise to be faithful, you can still promise to be honest. The moral here is: Don't promise what you cannot deliver—and remember to deliver what you *do* promise.

PARTNERS PAST

Tim and Annie's six-month relationship is over. Like many teenagers, both Tim and Annie will probably go on to have several, perhaps many, more relationships before they settle into one, long-term relationship or decide to remain single. Tim still harbors deep feelings for Annie, even though she doesn't feel the same way toward him. Given Tim's grief, does Annie have a responsibility not to flaunt her new relationship with Paul in front of Tim? For example, at a school dance or a party, should she refrain from kissing Paul or being physically demonstrative with him in front of Tim?

What do teenagers owe their "partners past"? Do they owe them privacy—keeping lips sealed about what transpired sexually? On the other hand, what information about their sexual past do they owe a new partner?

Kirsten was already emotionally involved with Ryan when she learned that he had fathered a baby a few years before. Should Ryan, or anyone else, have given her fair warning about his past? Or was it none of Kirsten's business? After all, she had her own sexual compass to navigate, and it didn't depend on Ryan's former girlfriends.

When someone hurts us, it is natural to feel anger toward them. And indeed, many relationships end on this note. While it is common to break up and say "let's remain friends," rising to that challenge can be difficult. What do we owe anyone who has broken off a relationship with us, especially someone who has hurt, deceived, or scorned us?

How you decide to deal with this issue depends on how you deal with the larger issue of forgiveness. Some people try to forgive all wrongs. Recently, on a television talk show, the mother of a murdered child forgave and befriended her son's murderer. While her nobility is truly inspirational, most people cannot stretch their righteousness so far.

Still, just as we can learn to control our emotions and our sex drive, we can restrain ourselves from spreading rumors or gossip about people who are no longer close to us, even if such treatment is not returned. As the old adage goes, "Never sink to their level." We can also follow the Golden Rule and treat them as we would like to be treated. Even if we fall short of such aspiration, we can strive for it and in the striving, acquire a fine moral habit and strengthen our character.

Much of our sexuality—some would say most of it—occurs between our ears and in our hearts. Trying to treat partners with respect and to show integrity in a relationship contributes a great deal to the sexual gratification each partner can get from the relationship, and to their character in general.

Some people find value in temporarily or permanently choosing to refrain from sexual contact. As in the issue of consent, holding up your end of the deal in a relationship—no matter what you choose to do or refrain from doing sexually—requires excellent communication, and mutual concern and empathy.

PRIVATE LIVES/PUBLIC FACES

During a routine undercover operation on the evening of July 26, 1991, police entered an adult movie theater in Sarasota, Florida, and arrested four people, including a 38-year-old man who had indecently exposed himself in order to twice masturbate while watching the porno movie *Catalina Tiger*. Paul Reubens, private citizen, dressed in shorts and a T-shirt and sporting a goatee, was unrecognizable as the clean-shaven comedian known as Peewee Herman, star of an Emmy Award–winning children's television show, "Peewee's Playhouse."

At the county detention facility, Reubens was charged, fingerprinted, and photographed. The next day, a reporter who recognized him from his mug shot quickly publicized the incident. Almost immediately, an ugly scandal erupted. Reubens's television show was canceled and his career shattered, leaving him emotionally distraught and greatly embarrassed.

Reubens's behavior is not an isolated incident. Other public figures have also appeared in a less than flattering limelight. Sol Wachtler, a respected New York State chief judge, was charged with an extortion scheme against a former lover. U.S. senator Bob Packwood of Oregon was charged with sexually harassing female employees, while earning a reputation as a champion of women's rights.

What private standards of sexual conduct should we expect our civil servants, teachers, clergy, and other role models and leaders to hold? Do we have a right to hold them to the highest of moral standards, or to conform to our own sexual moral compass?

Do their private lives interfere with their duties to the public or the people they serve? What responsibility do they have to avoid scandal that may bring shame and ill-repute to their families or their profession? Is their private sexual behavior any of our business? And finally, what rights and obligations do writers and reporters have to expose those lives or shield them from our public view?

FOOT SOLDIERS OF THE LORD AT FOUL PLAY

Some of the very people teaching us morality miss the moral mark themselves, shrinking from the ideals they are supposed to inspire in us. The rabbi of a large Jewish temple in the Midwest ignored one of the most basic commandments when he committed adultery and had an affair with someone. Only two years later, a Methodist minister who had befriended the rabbi committed the same sin. Each left his congregation, whose members were stunned and somewhat more cynical about the foot soldiers of the Lord.

When Jimmy Swaggart and James Bakker, wealthy television evangelists who had mesmerized millions of followers with their spiritual intonements and talk of family values, were literally caught with

their pants down—Swaggart with a prostitute and Bakker seducing his former secretary—the public's respect for the clergy diminished significantly.[1]

Besides those clergy who betray their constituents with their conduct, there are some who use their position to take advantage of people who look up to them, especially the young. Yet, don't people who have the trust of others have a duty to honor that trust? Despite repeated reports of sexual abuse and pedophilia by some members of the priesthood, officials of the Catholic church added another layer of wrongdoing by trying to cover up these scandals. Some accused priests were transferred to other parishes, with no warning to the new parishioners of the blemishes on their pasts.

THAT'S POLITICS

Reading from a roster of notable presidents that includes George Washington, Thomas Jefferson, Franklin D. Roosevelt, Dwight Eisenhower, and John F. Kennedy, adultery and sexual dalliance are commonplace in politics.[2]

When U.S. Senator Gary Hart was seeking the Democratic nomination for the nation's highest office in 1988, he was caught on a sailing trip with model Donna Rice. Both Hart and Rice denied any sexual misconduct, but the political damage had already occurred. Hart withdrew from the presidential race, accusing the media of unfair treatment—although when asked point-blank if he had ever committed adultery, he refused to answer.

Questions about sexual conduct arose again when then-presidental-candidate Bill Clinton was accused by Gennifer Flowers of having a twelve-year liaison with her. Like Hart, Clinton failed to quell suspicions of adultery.

Putting aside the (unanswered) question of whether a candidate's personal sexual history is relevant, Americans do care about these matters, as the intense media interest in both cases proves. Nearly 100 million viewers watched Clinton explain himself in a live interview on national television, while the story titillated the public for weeks. Still, Clinton was elected, by Americans who chose to overlook his private affairs when casting their votes.

Do journalists have the right to delve into our candidates' or leaders' private lives? And what right do we, the public, have to that information? In *Secrets*, ethicist Sissela Bok argues that the right to tell and our right to know is a "patently inadequate" excuse, and that while journalists can satisfy our curiosity, they must "pay special attention to individual privacy."[3] But what if marital indiscretions interfere with leadership?

If politicians lie to a spouse, what evidence do we have that they will be truthful to their public? Actually, we have evidence that regardless of what they tell or don't tell their spouses, politicians (and other human beings) may lie anyway. Peter Kim and James Patterson, authors of *The Day America Told the Truth*, found that the majority of people (91 percent) admit to lying regularly—although some people lie much more than others.[4]

Perhaps, as Katha Pollitt, writing for *The Nation*, suggests, the entire argument is specious. "Call me cynical," she says, "but I'll bet almost no male politicians are monogamous and almost none of their wives think they are. If we are going to hold politicians to strict moral standards," Pollitt suggests, "why not demand that they read books and write their own speeches?"[5]

OUT OF THE CLOSET

There are an estimated 3 to 5 million gay men, and another 600,000 to 1 million lesbians in America.[6] Many experts believe that the numbers are higher, because many gay Americans choose, albeit painfully, to "stay in the closet"[7] and keep their orientation private in order to protect themselves from job discrimination, social condemnation and ostracism, gay bashing, and the like.[8]

Allen Schindler, a twenty-one-year-old Navy sailor who was thought to be homosexual, was beaten to death so brutally that even his mother could not have identified him, had it not been for the tattoos she recognized on his arms.

After police raided Stonewall, a New York City gay bar on June 28, 1969, many homosexual activists voluntarily "came out" and revealed their homosexual or bisexual orientation. Soon, however, some homosexuals were being "outed" (their sexual orientation revealed against their will), sometimes by other homosexuals.

Michelangelo Signorile, gay author of a book about outing, claims that by throwing the light of publicity on celebrities and politicians who are gay, he is providing role models for the gay community. Another rationale decries the hypocrisy of homosexuals who take "anti-gay" positions in public.[9]

Following the vicious attack on liberalism, abortion, equal rights amendments, sex education, and homosexuality at the 1992 Republican Convention in Houston, Texas, John Schlafly, son of Phyllis Schlafly, champion of arch-conservative values, was outed. "I love my son," said Schlafly, scoffing at accusations of hypocrisy. "I'm the most tolerant person in the world."[10] This view was hardly supported by her relentless attacks on liberal lifestyles. But while there is little doubt about Schlafly's hypocrisy, was it fair to out her son, a private person? And when actress Jodie Foster appeared in *Silence of the*

Lambs, a movie that many in the gay community perceived as anti-gay, she, too, was outed as a lesbian.[11]

According to Richard Mohr, professor of philosophy and author of *Gay Ideas: Outing and Other Controversies*, outing is both a permissible and an expected consequence of living morally, but it should not be performed in order to provide role models, expose political hypocrisy, or to be vindictive. As Mohr explains, "Either being gay is okay, or it isn't. To accept the closet is to have absorbed society's view of gays, to accept insult so that one avoids harm. Life in the closet is morally debased and morally debasing. It frequently requires lying, but it always requires much more. . . . Allowing homosexuality to take its place as a normal part of the human sexual spectrum requires ceasing to treat it as a dirty little secret."[12]

Most gays disagree, and believe that involuntary outing is wrong.[13] Writing for the *New Republic,* Andrew Sullivan believes that people ought to choose their own moments of self-disclosure.[14]

If outing is sometimes fair, who has the right to do it—only a homosexual journalist, or any journalist? Some gay journalists believe that heterosexual journalists are wrong to out a homosexual, reasoning that a heterosexual can never understand what it is like to be gay in the first place or what is at stake in being outed.

Even though they may not have wanted it, some people are relieved to be out or to be outed. A case in point is that of the late Paul Monette, author of the award-winning autobiograph *Becoming a Man: Half a Life Story.* "I would not give up what the last seventeen years of being out have meant to me," Monette wrote. "It has been a joyous experience and that even includes the decade of

AIDS. I seem to be able to be as angry as I am and as despairing and still be a happy man, because now I am glad to be out."[15] But not everyone has had Monette's positive experience with outing.

Captain Dusty Pruitt voluntarily came out, but was clearly displeased with the reception she received. After revealing in a newspaper interview that she is a lesbian, Pruitt, an ordained minister and thirteen-year veteran of the Army Reserve, was forced into retirement. "It's sad," she said of the decision to discharge her from duty, "that the military wastes time bothering people about what they do in their private lives rather than what they do on duty."[16]

FALLING FROM GRACE

When the virtuous images of our heroes and heroines fail to hold up, the public is often quick to strip them of their status. Who gains or loses by such judgments?

Did young African-American girls lose a role model when Vanessa Williams (now a successful singer and actress), the first African-American crowned as Miss America, was forced to give up the title when nude photographs, taken long before her ascent to Miss America, emerged? Or did they gain a lesson in morality?

Was the public deprived of a good civil servant when U.S. Federal Judge Kendra Woods declined the nomination for U.S. attorney general, in part out of concern that her one-week tenure as a London Playboy bunny while studying in England would destroy public confidence in her ability to oversee the nation's legal work?

Even heroes and heroines may have feet of clay. From their public descents we can learn from their mistakes. When basketball star Magic Johnson admitted that he had contracted H.I.V. after an exceedingly reckless sex life, he hardly seemed worthy of being the role model he was. However, Magic had a positive influence on a number of people. According to a Maryland clinic that was conducting a study of sexual behavior when the announcement was made, the number of people in their study engaging in casual sex and multiple sex partners decreased substantially—from 1 in 3 to about 1 in 5.[17]

On a final note, what responsibility does the public have to give its leaders, role models, and public servants a second chance?

LET THE GOOD TIMES ROLL 13

So much is said to teenagers about the risks and sinfulness of sexual intercourse that many believe that the only thing adults have to say about sex is to fear or avoid it! And it is true that many parents do not believe their teenagers are ready for sexual intimacy, either for moral or practical reasons.

Many of these same parents are unwilling to let the schools teach sex education, or to offer teenagers public health clinics or condom distribution programs that would provide teenagers with protection against disease and pregnancy. At home, parents may be unapproachable, or too busy, or too uncomfortable to discuss sexuality.

All teenagers have the right to look forward to a gratifying sex life someday, if they desire one. For some teenagers, this will mean waiting until they are older or until they find a suitable partner, or until marriage. For others, it will mean postponing certain sexual behavior, such as intercourse, but experiencing a range of other behavior, including masturbation. And of course, as study after study finds, many teenagers, especially older ones, are doing everything their parents have done—and perhaps more.

In some societies, such options would never be available. In the United States, however, teenagers are, for the most part, free to determine for themselves when, where, and how they will let the good times roll.

Sex has two components—the release of sexual tension and emotional bonding. Thus, we can experience sex with our bodies and with our souls. Moreover, good sex takes on a different meaning with each experience. For some people, "good" means having any kind of sex—with anyone, any way, nearly anytime. As one of the characters in the movie *Threesome* said, "Sex is like pizza . . . even when it is bad, it is good."

For most people, however, the best sex happens when they can make an emotional attachment to another person and feel that what they are doing is right. Moral sex is consensual, responsible sex.

Many teenagers learn about sex from popular magazines, television, and movies, discussions with friends and parents, or conversations with older brothers and sisters. They also learn from or with their partners.

When adults have a problem enjoying sex, they have many places to seek help, including sex therapists, gynecologists, psychologists, urologists, and special clinics. Yet teenagers may have difficulty finding help. Few adults will advise teenagers about how to manage their sexual feelings, improve their sex lives, find gratification without in-

tercourse, and other concerns. Disabled youth, in particular, are treated as nonsexual, and are rarely taught alternative ways of gratifying themselves or their partners without full use of their bodies. And gay and lesbian teenagers often find it easier to shroud their sexual orientation in secrecy rather than risk disapproval from parents, peers, and others.

Furthermore, how many teenagers are taught to tolerate or respect moral viewpoints that are more conservative, or more liberal, than their own or those of their parents? How many perceive their parents as relics of an era of free love, or as straitlaced nonsexual beings?

Many people don't understand why their private sexual behavior is anyone else's business. Nor do they understand how their beliefs about sexual morality color their actual sexual experiences. Yet the connections, as we have seen throughout this book, are strongly linked.

MINDFUL CHOICES

We started this book with a look at the Spur Posse, a gang of boys who perceived sex as a game. We have concluded with basketball superstar Magic Johnson, hero to many. And we have looked at many private faces in between. The supreme test of sexual ethics, however, is not how we judge others, but how we judge ourselves. Even more essential, it is how we *behave*.

In pursuit of love, intimacy, or just momentary companionship, people sometimes compromise their moral standards. Compromising too often, they may find it impossible to return to their ideals.

Other people have one set of sexual standards for sober times and another set of standards while drinking or on drugs; one set for a person they respect and another for a person they hardly know. Still others trade a more conservative "home" compass for a looser, more liberal one on vacations and business trips. Not much moral footing here.

Ethics is about living and learning. There is no reason a person cannot upgrade his or her moral compass, learning from both ethical inquiry and experience alike. Neither a lurid past nor an accumulation of sexual partners, neither a bad reputation nor a bad experience should stop someone from improving his or her moral behavior or regaining confidence in the moral compass he or she once had.

People accustomed to being sexually exploited can regain their dignity, while people used to exploiting others for sex can learn respect and restraint. Sexual boundaries can be reset, and fear and inhibitions can be stripped away. And we can all improve our perspective on the sexual moral dilemmas and problems facing our society.

ENDNOTES

CHAPTER ONE

1. *Donahue*, April 15, 1993 (Journal Graphics, transcript #3798), 5.

2. John Schwartz, "Elders proves speaking one's mind carries risks," Cleveland *Plain Dealer* (Dec. 10, 1994).

3. Robert T. Michael, et al., *Sex in America* (New York: Little, Brown and Co., 1994), 138.

4. Ibid.

5. Ibid.

6. Ira L. Reiss, *An End to Shame* (Buffalo: Prometheus Books, 1990), 121; Mark Clements, "Sex in America Today," *Parade* (August 7, 1994), 4.

7. Among Americans aged 18 to 59, about 60 percent of men and 40 percent of women said they masturbated in the past year; one man in four and one woman in ten report masturbating at least once a week. Most of these adults have regular partners for sexual intercourse; Michael, *Sex in America*, 158.

8. The most conservative survey findings are that 3 percent to 10 percent of all American males are gay, while 1 percent to 3 percent of all females are lesbian. Many more Americans have had homosexual experiences, though they do not profess to be exclusively attracted to people of their own gender; Morton Hunt, *Gay* (New York: Farrar, Straus, Giroux, 1987), 105–106; Michael, *Sex in America*, Chapter 9, 169–183.

9. Michael, *Sex in America*, Chapter 12, 219–229.

10. In a 1988 national sample of 18 through 24-year-olds, 40 percent of the men and 15 percent of the women had had three or more sexual partners the previous year; over 80 percent had at least one partner; Reiss, *An End to Shame*, 121.

11. Michael, *Sex in America.*

12. Clements, "Sex in America Today," 6.

13. *Teens Talk About Sex: Adolescent Sexuality in the 90s*, survey by Roper Starch (New York: SIECUS, 1994), 24–25.

14. According to another study by The Guttmacher Institute, three-fourths of all boys and half of girls have experienced sexual intercourse by age 18.

15. Clements, "Sex in America Today," 6.

16. *Teens Talk About Sex*, 5.

17. "Chronic Disease and Health Promotion: 1990–1991 Youth Risk Behavior Surveillance System," U.S. Dept. of Health and Human Services, 45.

18. Jane Gross, "Sex Educators for Young See New Virtue in Chastity," *New York Times* (Jan. 16, 1994), A-1, 13.

19. "Chronic Disease and Health Promotion," 45; One-third of males and one-fifth of all females, however, initiate sex before age fifteen.

20. *Teens Talk*, 4.

21. *Sex in America*, 57.

CHAPTER TWO

1. Quoted in Lillian B. Rubin, *Erotic Wars* (New York: Harper-Collins, 1990), 13.

2. For a brief discussion of Catholic sexual ethics, see James P. Hanigan, *What Are They Saying about Sexual Morality?* (New York: Paulist Press, 1982), 18–20; for a discussion of Jewish sexual ethics, see David Baile, *Eros and the Jews* (New York: Basic Books, 1992); and for a source that summarizes all religious viewpoints on sexuality, see Geoffrey Parrinder, *Sex in the World's Religions* (New York: Oxford University Press, 1980).

3. Hanigan, *What Are They Saying?*

4. Baile, *Eros and the Jews*, 41–59.

5. For a brief overview of the entire history of sexual ethics, see Robert Baker and Frederick Elliston, eds., *Philosophy and Sex* (Buffalo: Prometheus Books, 1984), 11–36.

6. Ira L. Reiss, Ph.D., *Premarital Sexual Standards in America* (New York: Free Press, 1960), 53–58.

7. Helen E. Fisher, *Anatomy of Love* (New York: W.W. Norton, 1992), 49–51.

8. Reiss, *Premarital Sexual Standards*, 56.

9. Ibid., 57.

10. An excellent account of religion and sexual behavior in the nineteenth century is: Peter Gardella, *Innocent Ecstasy* (New York: Oxford University Press, 1985).

11. Gardella, *Innocent Ecstasy*; G.J. Barker-Benfield, *The Horrors of the Half-Known Life* (New York: Harper & Row, 1976).

12. Michael, *Sex in America*, 160.

13. Janus and Janus, *The Janus Report*, 11–12.

14. Ibid., 172–3.

15. Reiss, *An End to Shame*, 84.

16. Hunt, *Gay*, 105–6.

17. Kristin Luker, *Abortion & the Politics of Motherhood* (Berkeley, CA: University of California Press, 1984).

18. Rubin, *Erotic Wars*, 93.

19. People are more fearful of AIDS, and a substantial number are using condoms as a result. Still, neither the fear of AIDS, STD, or unwanted pregnancy has truly slowed down the sexual activity among mainstream Americans; telephone interview with Jean Burns, Ph.D., Kent State University, Department of Health Education (April 1993); telephone interview with Ira Reiss, Ph.D., University of Minnesota, Department of Sociology (April 2, 1993).

CHAPTER THREE

1. Michael, *Sex in America*, Chapter 3, 42–66.

2. Ibid., 231–2.

3. Hanigan, *What Are They Saying?*, 11.

4. Many contemporary theologians are rejecting traditional sexual ethics, including Charles E. Curran, James P. Hanigan, James B. Nelson, Carter Heyward, to name a few of those on the cutting edge of reform.

5. Findings from *The Girl Scouts' Survey on the Beliefs and Moral Values of America's Children* in 1989 indicated a significant correlation between religiosity and moral certainty; and a reverse correlation among adolescents who are not religious.

6. Manis Friedman, *Doesn't Anyone Blush Anymore?* (San Francisco: HarperCollins, 1990).

7. For a good discussion of the double standard, see Reiss, *Premarital Sex Standards in America,* 107–116; Rubin, *Erotic Wars*, 23–29; and Reiss, *An End to Shame*, 151–168.

8. Naomi Wolf, "Feminist Fatale," *The New Republic* (March 26, 1992), 24.

9. Ira Reiss, *Journey into Sexuality* (Englewood Cliffs, NJ: Prentice-Hall, 1986), 190–3.

10. Michael, *Sex in America*, 132–154.

11. Richard Wasserstrom, "Is Adultery Immoral?" *Philosphy and Sex*, Baker and Elliston, eds., 97.

12. Pamela Brubocker, interview, March 26, 1993.

13. Reiss, *An End to Shame*, 219–220.

14. Ibid.

15. Ibid.

CHAPTER FOUR

1. Michael, *Sex in America*, 223–5; According to this study, 22 percent of the women and 2 percent of the men had been forced to have

sex. And most of these people were either in love or married to the person who forced them.

2. *Sex and America's Teenagers* (New York: The Alan Guttmacher Institute of Planned Parenthood, 1994), 22.

3. Ibid.

4. The survey was conducted by the Center on Addiction and Substance Abuse at Columbia University, in 1994; reported by Thomas Brazaitis, "Smoking, drinking take new hits," Cleveland, *Plain Dealer* (June 8, 1994), 10-A. According to another study, 75 percent of men and 55 percent of women involved in acquaintance rapes had been drinking or taking drugs just before the attack; Robin Warshaw, *I Never Called It Rape* (New York: Harper & Row, 1988), 44.

5. Anna Quindlen, "The Legal Drug," *New York Times* (June 11, 1994), A-15.

6. "44 Percent of College Students are Binge Drinkers, Polls Say." *New York Times* (December 7, 1994); William Celes III, "Tradition on the Wane: College Drinking." *New York Times*, February 5, 1995, A1.

7. Ibid.

8. Michael, *Sex in America*, 223.

9. Martin Amis, quoted in Katie Roiphe, "Date Rape's Other Victim," *New York Times Magazine* (June 13, 1993), 40.

10. Carin Rubinstein, "Educators Urged to Address Sexual Harassment in School," *New York Times* (June 10, 1993).

11. Adrianne Le Blanc, "Harassment at School," *Seventeen* (May 1993), 134.

12. Melinda Henneberger and Michel Marriott, "For Some, Youthful Courting Has Become a Game of Abuse," *New York Times* (July 11, 1993).

13. Reiss, *An End to Shame*, 158–161.

14. "Sex-Trial Defense Lawyer Suggests Blaming Women's Parents," *New York Times* (Feb. 16, 1992).

15. "Sexual Violence and Safety," Antioch College report, 1994.

16. Ibid.

17. Jennifer Wolff, "Sex by the Rules," *Glamour* (May 1994), 258.

18. Ibid.

CHAPTER FIVE

1. Michael, *Sex in America*, Chapter 3.

2. Ibid., 44.

3. Ibid., 57.

4. Ibid., 55.

5. Scott Nearing, *The Super Race* (New York: B.W. Huebsch, 1912), 21.

6. Roselind Pollack Petchesky, *Abortion and Woman's Choice* (Boston: Northeastern University Press, 1984), 92.

7. Barry Mehler, "Eugenics in America: A Brief History," *Reform Judaism* (Winter 1994), 12.

8. Ibid.

9. Ronald Smother, "U.S. Moves to Oust Principal in Furor on Interracial Dating," *New York Times* (May 18, 1994), A-8.

10. Michael, *Sex in America*, 165.

11. Ken Kroll and Erica Levy Klein, *Enabling Romance* (New York: Harmony Books, 1992), 12.

12. Sam Maddox, "The Seven Year Itch," *New Mobility* (May/June 1994), 35.

13. Ibid., 38.

14. Victoria Megyesi, "I Don't Do Crips & Other Stories of Love and Lust," *New Mobility* (May/June 1994), 16.

15. Hanny Lightfoot-Klein, *Prisoners of Ritual: An Odyssey into Female Genital Circumcision in Africa* (Binghamton, NY: Harrington Park Press, 1989).

16. Marlise Simons, "Prosecutor Fighting Girl-Mutilation," *New York Times* (Jan. 23, 1993), A-4.

17. Ibid.

18. A. M. Rosenthal, "Female Genital Torture," *New York Times* (Oct. 12, 1993 and Dec. 24, 1993).

19. Simons, "Prosecutor Fighting Girl-Mutilation."

CHAPTER SIX

1. Stanley Grentz, *Sexual Ethics* (Dallas: Word Publishing, 1990), 188.

2. Helen E. Fisher, *Anatomy of Love* (New York: W. W. Norton, 1992), Chapter 1.

3. Ibid.

4. Ibid.

5. Ibid., Chapter 2.

6. Ibid.

7. Ibid. Also discussed in *Sex in America*, Chapters 3 and 4.

8. Michael, *Sex in America*, 42–66.

9. Fisher, *Anatomy of Love*, 53.

10. On the average, infatuation lasts anywhere from several months to several years; ibid., 57.

11. Ibid.

12. Ibid., 39.

13. Quoted in Grentz, *Sexual Ethics*, 182.

14. *Parade*, 4.

CHAPTER SEVEN

1. Norman Hearst, "Preventing Heterosexual Spread of AIDS: Are We Giving Patients the Best Advice?" *Journal of the American Medical Association* (April 22/29, 1988).

2. "Chronic Disease and Health," 45.

3. *Sex and America's Teenagers*, 38.

4. "Sex and Consequences," *New York Times* (April 7, 1993).

5. *Sex and America's Teenagers*, 34–35.

6. U.S. Centers for Disease Control, telephone interview (March 23, 1993).

7. *Sex and America's Teenagers*, 43.

8. Ibid., 45.

9. *Sex and America's Teenagers,* 50.

10. Ibid., 45.

11. Only 11 percent of pregnant teens marry the father; one-third of these marriages end in divorce within five years; "Sex and America's Teenagers," 60.

12. "Sex and America's Teenagers," 58–59.

13. Ibid., 22.

14. Ibid., 28, 42.

15. Interviewed by Laura Morice, "He's having a baby," *YM* (May 1993), 59.

16. Joe Frolik, "The Out-of-wedlock baby boom," *Plain Dealer* (Nov. 28, 1993); 80 percent of all teenage mothers giving birth are living in poverty or low-income households, *Sex and America's Teenagers*, 74–75.

17. Ibid., 45.

18. Nell Bernstein, "Learning to Love," *Mother Jones* (Jan/Feb 1995), 49.

19. Ibid., 30.

20. Ibid.

21. Reiss, *An End to Shame*, 116.

22. "Sex and America's Teenagers," 31.

23. Daniel Goldman, "Teenagers Called Shrewd Judges of Risk," *New York Times* (March 2, 1993).

24. Ibid.

25. Ibid.

26. Reiss, *An End to Shame*, 125–127.

27. The average length of a sex education program is only seven hours per school year; Bernstein, "Learning to Love," 48.

28. Peter C. Scales, "Just Say Yes to Sex Education," *Today* (Spring 1993), 7.

29. Cindi Lieve, "Women, AIDS, Condoms and Confidence," *Glamour* (May 1994), 180.

30. Neville Blakemore and Neville Blakemore, Jr., give an excellent account of sexual ethics in law, medicine, and religion in their book, *The Serious Side of Sex* (Louisville, KY: Nevbet, 1991), 21.

31. A good account of sodomy laws is in Wayne C. Bartee and Alice Fleetwood Bartee, *Litigating Morality* (New York: Praeger, 1992), 31–55; and Richard Mohr, *Gay Ideas* (Boston: Beacon Press, 1992), 54–86.

CHAPTER EIGHT

1. Ruth Westheimer and Louis Leiberman, *Sex and Morality: Who is Teaching Our Sex Standards?* (New York: Harcourt, Brace, Jovanovich, 1988), 77–9.

2. Ibid.

3. John Duffy, "Sex, Society, Medicine: An Historical Comment," reprinted from Earl E. Shelp, ed., *Sexuality and Medicine* (D. Reidel Publishers, 1987), Vol. II, 70.

4. Westheimer and Leiberman, *Sex and Morality*, 78.

5. Janus and Janus, *The Janus Report*, 43–4.

6. Actually, the median age is 24.5 for women and 26.5 for men. U.S. Census Bureau, reported in Steven A. Holmes, "Birthrate for Unwed Women Up to 70% Since '83, Study Says," *New York Times* (July 24, 1994), A-7.

7. *The Janus Report*, 385.

8. "True Love Waits for Some Teen-Agers," *New York Times* (June 21, 1993)

9. Sherri Kohn, telephone interview (May 15, 1993).

10. Renee Lucas Wayne, "Abstinence with attitude," *Beacon Journal* (Akron, Ohio) (May 11, 1994), C-1.

11. Ibid.

12. Grentz, *Sexual Ethics*, 287.

13. Karen Bouris, *The First Time* (Berkeley, CA: Conari Press, 1993), 183.

14. Ibid.

15. Ibid, 12.

16. Ibid, 185.

17. "Teens Talk About Sex," 4.

CHAPTER NINE

1. Thomas A. Nazario, *In Defense of Children: Understanding the Rights, Needs, and Interests of the Child* (New York: Charles Scribner's Sons, 1988), 393.

2. Linda Greenhouse, "A Divided Supreme Court Ends the Term With A Bang: Abortion," *New York Times* (July 1, 1990); *Parental Notice Laws*, pamphlet, ACLU (1986).

3. Marty Klein, *Your Sexual Secrets* (New York: Dutton, 1988), 56.

4. Sissela Bok, *Secrets: On the Ethics of Concealment and Revelation* (New York: Vintage Books, 1989), 25.

5. Ibid., 18.

CHAPTER TEN

1. Alison Lurie, *The Language of Clothing* (New York: Random House, 1981), 3.

2. "The Naked Guy Meets Naked Truth," *San Francisco Chronicle* (Jan. 29, 1993); "Radical Cheek," *People* (Dec. 21, 1992), 101.

3. "Courage in the Raw," *Backpacker* (Oct. 1990), 14.

4. Charles Leerhern, "The Naked and the Dread," *Newsweek* (Sept. 10, 1990), 60.

5. Larry Rohter, "Florida Approves Public Breast-Feeding, *New York Times* (Mar. 4, 1993), A-8.

6. Anna Quindlen, "To Feed or Not to Feed," *New York Times* (May 25, 1994), A-13.

7. *Sonja Live* (July 23, 1993, transcript #99), 9.

8. "Teens Talk About Sex," 22.

9. Judith Martin, *Common Courtesy* (New York: Atheneum, 1985).

CHAPTER ELEVEN

1. Kroll and Klein, *Enabling Romance*.

2. Michael, *Sex in America*, 192.

3. Ibid., 192–3.

4. Ibid., 195.

5. Michael J. Wreen, "What's Really Wrong with Adultery?" *The Philosophy of Sex*, 2d ed., Alan Soble, ed. (Savage, MD: Rowan & Littlefield, 1991), 179–186.

CHAPTER TWELVE

1. Gallup Poll, 1989.

2. Dennis Prager, "Faith Unto Office," *The National Review* (July 6, 1992), 47.

3. Bok, *Secrets*, 284, 287.

4. James Patterson and Peter Kim. *The Day America Told the Truth* (New York: Prentice-Hall, 1991), 46.

5. Katha Pollitt, "Clinton's Affair?" *The Nation* (February 24, 1992), 221.

6. In the dozen largest U.S. cities, 10.2 percent of the men and 2.1 percent of the women report having a sexual partner of their own sex in the past year; in rural areas, those findings drop to only 1 percent of the men and six-tenths of 1 percent of the women; reported by David W. Dunlap, "Gay Survey Raises a New Question," *New York Times* (Oct. 18, 1994), A-10; also corroborated in *Sex in America*, Chapter 9.

7. Hunt, *Gay*, 12–13. Some gay activists claim that there are more than twice, or even three times, that number of gay people. Furthermore, more Americans have *reported* having had a homosexual experience than report being homosexual. According to several studies, many more people have experienced gay sex than consider themselves exclusively gay.

8. Estimates vary regarding the number of gays who keep their homosexuality a secret, but they usually range from two-thirds to nine-tenths of all gays, according to Hunt, *Gay*, 90. For an excellent discussion of the ethics of outing, see Mohr, *Gay Ideas* (New York: Random House, 1993).

9. Reported by Alexander Cockburn, "Beat the Devil: The Old In/Out," *The Nation* (Aug. 26/Sept. 2, 1991), 220.

10. Schlafly's Son: Out of the G.O.P. Closet," *Newsweek* (Sept. 28, 1992), 18.

11. Signorile, *Queer in America* (New York: Random House, 1993), 89.

12. Mohr, *Gay Ideas*, 12.

13. Ibid., 11.

14. Andrew Sullivan, "Washington Diarist: Sleeping with the Enemy," *The New Republic* (Sept. 9, 1991), 43.

15. Paul Monette, "The Politics of Silence," *New York Times* (Mar. 7, 1993), Op-Ed.

16. Nancy Gibbs, "Marching Out of the Closet," *Time* (Aug. 9, 1991), 14.

17. *New York Times* (Jan. 29, 1993), A-7.

GLOSSARY

Abstinence: voluntarily refraining from sexual intercourse

Adultery: when a married person has sex with someone other than his or her spouse

Anal sex: insertion of the penis into a partner's rectum

Bestiality: also called zoophilia; a sexual act with an animal

Bisexuality: being able to get sexual satisfaction from persons of either gender

Casual sex: sex that lacks an emotional commitment to or affection for one's partner

Celibacy: complete absence of all sexual activity, including masturbation and sexual thoughts

Character: the overall combination of a person's moral traits

Chaste: not engaging in sexual intercourse; celibate

Chauvinism, male: a superior attitude that some men adopt toward women

Circumcision, female: removal of the clitoris; may also include removal of other sexual parts, such as the labia, and the stitching closed of practically all of the vaginal opening

Circumcision, male: removal of the fold of skin surrounding the tip of the penis

Clitorectomy: removal of the tip of the clitoris or the entire clitoris

Coitus: intercourse

Condom: a rubberized or animal skin shield for the penis or the vagina

Consent, sexual, and consensual sex: mutual agreement to a sexual act

Date rape: forced sex that occurs between people who know one another and are together socially

Diaphragm: a rubberized shield that covers a woman's cervix in order to prevent pregnancy

Ejaculation: a discharge of seminal fluid, which may or may not contain semen, during a male's orgasm

Erection: the stiffening of a penis due to an increase in blood

Ethics: the study of morality; learning about right and wrong, and good and bad

Etiquette: socially acceptable conduct

Eugenics: a branch of genetic science that is concerned with genetic superiority

Exhibitionism: compulsive act of publicly exposing genitals for the purpose of sexual arousal

Extramarital sex: when a married person has sexual relations with someone other than the spouse

Fantasy, sexual: erotic thoughts that increase sexual arousal and pleasure

Fetish: sexual fixation on an object, concept, or body part, such as the foot

Foreplay: sexual acts before or instead of intercourse

Fornication: sexual intercourse between unmarried persons

Free love: having sex with anyone desired; usually includes a variety of partners

Gay: having a sexual orientation toward persons of the same gender

Guilt: remorse for some act

Immoral: in ethics, wrong or bad behavior

Impotence: inability to have or maintain an erection

Incest: sexual activity between members of the same family

Intolerance: disrespect for a different viewpoint or behavior

Lesbian: a female who desires sex with other females

Libido: a person's sexual drive and energy

Masturbation: stimulation of the genitals for sexual gratification; usually refers to self-stimulation. *See also* mutual masturbation

Monogamy: remaining sexually faithful to the partner to whom you have made an emotional or marital commitment

Moral agency, moral autonomy: having the ability and freedom to make one's own moral decisions

Moral ambiguity: confusion or uncertainty about what is moral or immoral in a situation

Moral awareness: realizing that a situation is morally right or wrong, and that certain situations have ethical considerations

Moral compass: the moral principles and values used to determine how to live morally

Moral conflict: knowing what is right, but struggling over whether or not to do it

Mutual masturbation: sexual partners' stimulation of each other's genitals

Nonmarital sex: sex between two people not married to each other

Nudist: a person who chooses to abstain from wearing clothing in public or during activities where most people routinely dress

Oral sex: mouth contact with the penis or vagina

Orgasm: highly pleasurable, climactic response during sex

Outing: making public the sexual orientation of a homosexual; if done without the person's permission, he or she has been "outed."

Petting: sexual activity that is more intimate than simply kissing, but that stops short of intercourse

Pluralism: when many viewpoints coexist in a society

Premarital sex: sex that occurs before a person is married. Since many people remain single for a long time or never marry, the term "nonmarital sex" is often used instead.

Premature ejaculation: when a male reaches orgasm too soon to satisfy his partner sexually

Procreation: producing children

Prostitution: sexual services in exchange for money

Prudery: extreme sexual modesty

Recreational sex: casual sex or sex between two people who are not committed to each other for the long term

Sadomasochism: sexual gratification by causing or receiving pain or threat of pain

Sexual assault: forcing sex on someone who has not consented

Sexual ethics: studying sexuality with respect to morality

Sexual orientation: a person's sexual attraction; heterosexual (opposite sex attraction); homosexual (same-sex attraction); and bisexual (attracted to both genders)

Shame: feeling remorse for something done that would disappoint or distress others

Sodomy: anal intercourse or using one's mouth to sexually stimulate a partner's sexual organs

STD: sexually transmitted disease

Temperance: the ability to be in control of oneself and put limits on sexual behavior

Testosterone: a male hormone that contributes to the male sex drive

Tolerance: being fair toward others who are different, and being open-minded about different moral viewpoints

Virginity: never having had sexual intercourse

Virtue: moral excellence, or a particular commendable trait, such as courage, wisdom, or kindness

Voyeurism: seeking sexual satisfaction from seeing others' sexual organs or sexual acts.

BIBLIOGRAPHY

Ard, Ben Neal, Jr. *Rational Sex Ethics*. New York: Peter Lang, 1989.

Avna, Joan, and Diana Walty. *Celibate Wives*. Chicago: Contemporary Books, 1992.

Biale, David. *Eros and the Jews*. New York: Basic Books, HarperCollins, 1992.

Baker, Robert and Frederick Elliston, eds. *Philosophy and Sex*. Buffalo: Prometheus Books, 1984.

Barker-Benfield, G. J. *The Horrors of the Half-Known Life: Male Attitudes Toward Women and Sexuality in Nineteenth-Century America*. New York: Harper & Row, 1976.

Bartee, Wayne C., and Alice Fleetwood Bartee. *Litigating Morality*. New York: Praeger Publishers, 1992.

Blakemore, Neville, and Neville Blakemore, Jr. *The Serious Side of Sex*. Louisville: The Nevbet Company, 1991.

Bok, Sissela. *Secrets*. New York: Vintage Books, 1984.

Brown, Gabrielle. *The New Celibacy*. New York: McGraw-Hill, 1989.

Cahill, Lisa Sowle. *Between the Sexes: Foundations for Christian Ethics of Sexuality*. Philadelphia: Fortress Press, 1985.

Carrera, Michael A. *The Language of Sex*. New York: Facts on File, 1982.

Costello, John. *Virtue Under Fire: How World War II Changed Our Social and Sexual Attitudes*. Boston: Little, Brown, and Co.,1985.

Curran, Charles E. *Issues in Sexual and Medical Ethics*. Notre Dame, Indiana: University of Notre Dame Press, 1978.

Dryfoos, Joy G. *Putting the Boys in the Picture*. Santa Cruz: Network Publications, 1988.

Dworkin, Andrea. *Intercourse*. New York: The Free Press Macmillan, 1987.

Ellis, Albert. *Sex Without Guilt*. North Hollywood: Wilshire Book Co., 1966.

Ehrenriech, Barbara, and Deirdre English. *For Her Own Good: 150 Years of Experts' Advice to Women*. Garden City, NY: Anchor Press, 1978.

Fisher, Helen E. *Anatomy of Love*. New York: W.W. Norton, 1992.

Friedman, Manis. *Doesn't Anyone Blush Anymore?* Edited by Jena Morris Breningstall. San Francisco: Harper SanFrancisco, 1990.

Fromer, Margot Joan. *Ethical Issues in Sexuality & Reproduction*. St. Louis: The C.V. Mosby Co., 1983.

Gardella, Peter. *Innocent Ecstasy: How Christianity Gave America an Ethic of Sexual Pleasure*. New York: Oxford University Press, 1985.

Glover, Jonathan. "It Makes No Difference Whether or Not I Do It." In *Applied Ethics,* edited by Peter Singer. New York: Oxford University Press, 1986.

Grentz, Stanley. *Sexual Ethics: A Biblical Perspective*. Dallas: Word Publishing, 1990.

Hampshire, Stuart. *Morality and Conflict*. Cambridge, Massachusetts: Harvard University Press, 1983.

Harriss, John, ed. *The Family*. New York: Oxford University Press, 1991.

Hartment, William, Marilyn Fithian, and Donald Johnson. *Nudist Society*. Los Angeles: Elysium Growth Press, 1991.

Heyward, Carter. *Touching Our Strength*. San Francisco: Harper & Row, 1989.

Janus, Samuel S., and Cynthia L. Janus. *The Janus Report on Sexual Behavior*. New York: John Wiley & Sons, Inc., 1993.

Kilpatrick, William. *Why Johnny Can't Tell Right from Wrong*. New York: Simon and Schuster, 1992.

Klein, Marty. *Your Sexual Secrets*. New York, E.P. Dutton, 1988.

Klein, Susan Shurberg, ed. *Sex Equity and Sexuality in Education*. Albany: State University of New York Press, 1992.

Koop, C. Everett. "Public Health and Private Ethics." Lecture at the Children's Health Center, Minneapolis, October 17, 1986.

Lawler, Ronald, et. al. *Catholic Sexual Ethics*. Huntington, Indiana: Our Sunday Visitor, 1985.

Leone, Bruno, and M. Teresa O'Neill. *Sexual Values: Oppos-*

ing Viewpoints. St. Paul: Greenhaven Press, 1983.

McCarthy, Donald G., and Edward J. Bayer. *Critical Sexual Issues.* St. Louis: The Pope John Center, 1983.

Michael, Robert T., et al. *Sex in America.* New York: Little, Brown and Co., 1994.

Nelson, James B. *Embodiment.* New York: The Pilgrim Press, 1978.

Parrinder, Geoffrey. *Sex in the World's Religions.* New York: Oxford University Press, 1980.

Patterson, James, and Peter Kim. *The Day America Told the Truth.* New York: Prentice-Hall, 1991.

Rubin, Lillian B. *Erotic Wars: What Happened to the Sexual Revolution?* New York: Farrar, Straus & Giroux, 1990.

Russell, Bertrand. *On Ethics, Sex, and Marriage.* Edited by Al Seckel. Buffalo: Prometheus Books, 1987.

Sex and America's Teenagers. New York: The Alan Guttmacher Institute of Planned Parenthood, 1994.

Schur, Edwin M. *The Americanization of Sex.* Philadelphia: Temple University Press, 1988.

Scruton, Roger. *Sexual Desire: A Moral Philosophy of the Erotic.* New York: The Free Press, 1988.

Siskin, Bernard, and Jerome Staller. *What Are the Chances?: Risks, Odds & Likelihood in Everyday Life.* New York: Crown Publishing, 1989.

Soble, Alan, ed. *The Philosophy of Sex.* Savage, Maryland: Rowman & Littlefield, 1991.

Stein, Harry. *Ethics (and Other Liabilities).* New York: St. Martin's Press, 1982.

"Stopping Sexual Assault in Marriage." Pamphlet. New York: The Center for Constitutional Rights, 1986.

Ulanov, Ann Belford, et al. *Men and Women: Sexual Ethics in Turbulent Times.* Cambridge, MA: Cowley Publications, 1989.

U.S. Dept. of Health and Human Services. *Sexually Transmitted Disease: Surveillance, 1991.* Atlanta: Centers for Disease Control, 1992.

Vaughan, Peggy. *The Monogamy Myth.* New York: Newmarket Press, 1989.

Welch, Leslee. *The Complete Book of Sexual Trivia.* New York: Carol Publishing Group, 1992.

Westheimer, Ruth, and Louis Leiberman. *Sex and Morality: Who is Teaching Our Sex Standards?* New York: Harcourt, Brace, Jovanovich, 1988.

Wile, Ira S., ed. *The Sex Life of the Unmarried Adult.* New York: Garden City Publishing Co., 1940.

FOR FURTHER READING

Baile, David. *Eros and the Jews.* New York: Basic Books, HarperCollins, 1992.

Baker, Robert, and Frederick Elliston, eds. *Philosophy and Sex.* Buffalo: Prometheus Books, 1984.

Barker-Benfield, G. J. *The Horrors of the Half-Known Life: Male Attitudes Toward Women and Sexuality in Nineteenth-Century America.* New York: Harper & Row, 1976.

Bartee, Wayne C., and Alice Fleetwood Bartee. *Litigating Morality.* New York: Praeger Publishers, 1992.

Blakemore, Neville, and Neville Blakemore, Jr. *The Serious Side of Sex.* Louisville: The Nevbet Company, 1991.

Cahill, Lisa Sowle. *Between the Sexes: Foundations for Christian Ethics of Sexuality.* Philadelphia: Fortress Press, 1985.

Costello, John. *Virtue Under Fire: How World War II Changed Our Social and Sexual Attitudes.* Boston: Little, Brown & Co., 1985.

Curren, Charles E. *Issues in Sexual and Medical Ethics.* Notre Dame, Indiana: University of Notre Dame Press, 1978.

Fisher, Helen E. *Anatomy of Love.* New York: W.W. Norton, 1992.

Gardella, Peter. *Innocent Ecstasy: How Christianity Gave America an Ethic of Sexual Pleasure.* New York: Oxford University Press, 1985.

Grentz, Stanley. *Sexual Ethics: A Biblical Perspective.* Dallas, Texas: Word Publishing, 1990.

Janus, Samuel S. and Cynthia L. Janus. *The Janus Report on Sexual Behavior.* New York: John Wiley & Sons, Inc., 1993.

Klein, Marty. *Your Sexual Secrets.* New York: E.P. Dutton, 1988.

Lawler, Ronald, et al. *Catholic Sexual Ethics*. Huntington, Indiana: Our Sunday Visitor, 1985.

Leone, Bruno, and M. Teresa O'Neill. *Sexual Values: Opposing Viewpoints*. St. Paul: Greenhaven Press, 1983.

Michael, Robert T., et al. *Sex in America*. New York: Little, Brown & Co., 1994.

Parrinder, Geoffrey. *Sex in the World's Religions*. New York: Oxford University Press, 1980.

Rubin, Lillian B. *Erotic Wars: What Happened to the Sexual Revolution?* New York: Farrar, Straus & Giroux, 1990.

Soble, Alan, ed. *The Philosophy of Sex*. Savage, Maryland: Rowman & Littlefield, 1991.

Terkel, Susan Neiburg. *Ethics*. New York: Lodestar, 1992.

Westheimer, Ruth, and Louis Leiberman. *Sex and Morality: Who is Teaching Our Sex Standards?* New York: Harcourt Brace Jovanovich, 1988.

INDEX

ABOUT THE AUTHOR

Susan Neiburg Terkel grew up in Pennsylvania and was educated at Cornell University, where she earned a degree in child development and family relationships. For the past few years, she has been exploring the subject of ethics in a variety of contexts. She contributed to a college ethics textbook and is the author of several well-received books for young people, including *Abortion: Facing the Issues, Understanding Child Custody, Understanding Cancer* (written with Marlene K. Lupiloff-Brazz), and *Colonial Medicine*, all published by Franklin Watts. She has also written *Ethics*, and *Feeling Safe, Feeling Strong: A Book About Sexual Abuse.*

Ms. Terkel is now working on a book about drug policy and is serving as consultant for an encyclopedia of ethics. She lives in Ohio with her husband and three children.